RIDE AROUND MISSOURI

Shelby's Great Raid 1863

SEAN McLACHLAN

First published in Great Britain in 2011 by Osprey Publishing,
Midland House, West Way, Botley, Oxford, OX2 0PH, UK
44–02 23rd St, Suite 219, Long Island City, NY 11101, USA

E-mail: info@ospreypublishing.com

A CIP catalog record for this book is available from the British Library

Print ISBN: 978 1 84908 429 1
PDF e-book ISBN: 978 1 84908 430 7
EPUB e-book ISBN: 978 1 84908 890 9

Page layout by Bounford.com
Index by Sandra Shotter
Typeset in Sabon
Maps by Bounford.com
Originated by United Graphics Pte., Singapore
Printed in China through Worldprint Ltd.

11 12 13 14 15   10 9 8 7 6 5 4 3 2 1

Osprey Publishing is supporting the Woodland Trust, the UK's leading
woodland conservation charity, by funding the dedication of trees.

www.ospreypublishing.com

DEDICATION

For Almudena, my wife, and Julián, my son.

ACKNOWLEDGEMENTS

The author wishes to thank the following for their generous assistance: Rex
Dickson and Caitlin Lenon for their hospitality; the Kneighborhood Knights
for chess and conversation; the staff of the State Historical Society of
Missouri and the Western Historical Manuscript Department for finding
photos and primary documents; and Shelby's 5th Missouri Cavalry for their
excellent reenactment photos and for keeping the memory of the Iron
Brigade alive. Shelby's 5th is one of the oldest mounted reenactment units
in the Trans-Mississippi and is always looking for new members. Contact
cavscott@aol.com for information. Thanks to Missouri artist Andy Thomas
for permission to use two of his excellent painting. Prints of these paintings
are available from www.andythomas.com.

AUTHOR'S NOTE

All photos credited (LoC) are courtesy the Library of Congress, Photo and
Print Division.

CONTENTS

INTRODUCTION

Joseph Orville Shelby was born to a rich planter family in Lexington, Kentucky, on December 12, 1830. One of his childhood friends was John Hunt Morgan, who would grow up to be another famous Confederate cavalry raider. Shelby enjoyed the privileges of wealth and education, but unlike many young men of his social station, he never joined the army or even the local militia. In fact, he had no military experience whatsoever until he heard his first shot fired in anger. In 1849 he moved to the Missouri River town of Lexington to work at his stepfather's hemp factory. Before being banned for its recreational uses, hemp was an important cash crop in both Kentucky and Missouri – the fiber could be turned into rope, cloth, medicine, paper, and many other products. It was also closely linked to the cotton industry, which required huge amounts of cordage to tie up cotton bales. Both industries involved hard manual labor and relied on large numbers of slaves.

Joseph Orville Shelby. (Courtesy State Historical Society of Missouri)

In 1852 Shelby inherited a large sum of money and moved west to the small town of Waverly, which like Lexington was a growing river port earning wealth from the thriving steamboat trade on the Missouri River. Here he bought land to raise hemp, wheat, cattle, corn, and hogs. Like his father and stepfather before him, he also raised blooded horses. Shelby's horses became famous for their fine breeding, and Shelby himself was renowned as an excellent rider. He also built a ropewalk where slaves twisted hemp fibers into cord for the cotton and shipping industry.

By the mid 1850s, Shelby enjoyed peace and prosperity, but the stability was not to last. To the west of Missouri in the Kansas Territory, a debate was heating up over whether Kansas would become a slave state or a free state. The Kansas–Nebraska Act of 1854 dictated that these two territories would decide the issue by popular vote when their time came to apply for statehood. Everyone assumed that the more northerly Nebraska would vote against slavery, but

Kansas was a different matter. The rolling prairie of western Missouri, with its patchwork of woodland, was the same in nature as that in eastern Kansas. Since Kansas shared Missouri's geography, Missourians assumed they would settle it once all the good land in their own state had been taken – they saw Kansas as the logical extension of Missouri. Some Northerners had other ideas. The New England Emigrant Aid Society financed Northern abolitionists to move to Kansas. Many came armed with Sharps rifles, the finest of their day, supplied by abolitionists themselves.

Jennison's jayhawkers raiding a Missouri farm. Raids by Free-State Kansans into Missouri and pro-slavery bushwhackers into Kansas started the violence of the Civil War. J.O. Shelby was at the forefront of the bushwhacker movement and admitted to killing Kansans, although he later regretted his actions. (LoC)

In response, leading Missourians founded the Blue Lodge, a quasi-Masonic organization dedicated to making Kansas a slave state. Shelby was one of its leading members. When Kansas held elections for a Congressional delegate in December 1854, Missourians crossed the border to vote and managed to get a pro-slavery man elected. The more important elections for the territorial legislature came on March 30, 1855. Shelby and other Blue Lodge leaders led thousands across the border. There were no precise rules as to residency requirements for voting, and the crowds of armed and often drunk Missourians persuaded officials that presence equaled residence. At the little village of Switzer's Creek, only 53 eligible voters were listed in the poll books, yet the village cast 607 votes.

When Union troops and German militia arrested the Missouri State Guardsmen camped outside St. Louis on May 10, 1861, a secessionist crowd threw stones at them. One rioter shot a soldier, at which point the troops fired volleys into the crowd. This incident polarized Missouri's population and hastened the march to war. (LoC)

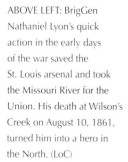

ABOVE LEFT: BrigGen Nathaniel Lyon's quick action in the early days of the war saved the St. Louis arsenal and took the Missouri River for the Union. His death at Wilson's Creek on August 10, 1861, turned him into a hero in the North. (LoC)

This blatant election rigging set off a firestorm of controversy. The Northern press railed against the Missourians, while the Southern press rejoiced. New waves of abolitionist immigrants entered Kansas, and soon Missouri "bushwhackers" or "border ruffians" began raiding Kansas, burning abolitionist presses and killing Kansans. Kansas "jayhawkers" or "red legs" rode into Missouri, murdering slave owners and taking slaves back to Kansas to free them. Shelby led some of the bushwhacker raids and admitted to killing Kansans during what became known as "Bleeding Kansas." He was not immune to reprisals, however. When his sawmill burned down, he suspected it to be the work of jayhawkers. Violence begat violence, and it took some time before the army could contain the situation, and even then they only achieved partial success.

This first chapter of the Civil War continued until South Carolina seceded on December 20, 1860, setting off a wave of secession across the South and the foundation of the Confederacy. The Civil War had now entered its second chapter. Missouri's governor, Claiborne Fox Jackson, wanted Missouri to join the Confederacy. Much of the legislature and rural population agreed, but he faced strong opposition from cities such as St. Louis, Columbia, and Kansas City (this border city, despite its name, is mostly in Missouri). In addition, large numbers of German immigrants had settled in St. Louis and along the Missouri River and they were strongly abolitionist. The majority of Missourians wanted to avert war, but soon events in St. Louis forced them to take sides. When the State Guard gathered in St. Louis, local commander Capt Nathaniel Lyon suspected them of planning to capture the Federal arsenal. He brought out the German militia and Federal soldiers to arrest them on May 10, 1861. The outnumbered State Guard quickly surrendered and Lyon's men marched them into town. Angry secessionist civilians thronged the streets. The crowd soon turned into a riot, with people throwing rocks at the soldiers. When someone pulled out a pistol and shot a soldier, the troops responded with several volleys. By the time the smoke cleared, one soldier and 27 civilians lay dead.

Shelby witnessed the whole thing. He had traveled to St. Louis to help his friend John Hunt Morgan, who was in Kentucky raising men for the Southern cause and wanted 100,000 musket caps. Shelby bought them from a pro-Southern gun dealer and shipped them to Morgan hidden in the earth of flower pots, with lilacs, dahlias, and roses put on top. Then he hurried back to Waverly to set up his own command.

After the St. Louis massacre, Governor Jackson easily passed a resolution to secede from the Union. Peace overtures between the two sides soon fell apart. Jackson feared that he would be overrun in the state capital of Jefferson City, exposed as it was in the center of the state, and moved west to Boonville, where various units of the secessionist State Guard were converging. Lyon, having just been promoted to brigadier-general by President Lincoln, gathered 1,700 men and sailed up to Boonville to catch them. He defeated them on June 17, 1861, in a brief engagement that was one of the earliest land battles of the war. While the skirmish was an easy victory for Lyon, it had repercussions far beyond its size. The Missouri River fell into Union hands, cutting the state in half and allowing Union forces to move quickly across it.

Shelby wasn't there for the fiasco. He was home organizing the Lafayette County Cavalry, 43 men who would later become the nucleus of his famous Iron Brigade. All were mounted and equipped out of Shelby's own pocket. Like him, many were veterans of Bleeding Kansas. He told them they must, "fight for the South until she was free, for twenty years if necessary." Shelby soon joined the State Guard in southwest Missouri, where they had retreated and were gathering recruits. Their commander was MajGen Sterling Price, a hero of the Mexican–American War and former governor of Missouri.

OPPOSITE RIGHT: Col Henry Almstedt of the 2nd Missouri Artillery spent much of his time commanding small garrisons and struggling with rebel guerrillas. A letter to his superior dated September 15, 1862, reveals some typical troubles. "I am not strong enough to secure the place against a possible nightly surprise. Naturally the town is open from all sides; to confine the entrances on certain main roads I have made an abatis on the whole circuit. With my present force of infantry I cannot advance the pickets beyond this abatis, and I cannot make these pickets stronger than three men each; their distance from camp is not more than 500 yards the nearest and 800 yards the remotest. A nightly attack on those pickets will leave us scarcely sufficient time to get ready for the fight." (LoC)

Col Madison Miller of the 18th Missouri Infantry stands by his horse. Since Missouri was not considered a state in rebellion, Lincoln's 1863 Emancipation Proclamation didn't apply to it. The man holding the horse may have been a slave, and remained so until a state convention freed all slaves in Missouri on January 11, 1865. The 18th served in Missouri until March 1862, when like many other units, both North and South, it was transferred east of the Mississippi. It wouldn't see home again until the end of the war. Miller was declared missing at the battle of Shiloh. (LoC)

The battle of Wilson's Creek on August 10, 1861, made BrigGen Nathaniel Lyon a Union martyr and taught J.O. Shelby the value of cannons after he charged without artillery support and was bloodily repulsed. (LoC)

Shelby was awarded the rank of captain despite his lack of military training. Being a gentleman and showing up with a command already organized was enough to get a good rank in those early days of the war.

Union troops were on the move, and on July 5 Shelby fought his first battle. A Union detachment under the experienced German-American officer Col Franz Sigel clashed with the rebels outside the town of Carthage. The Union side had a little over a thousand well-trained men. The rebels had four times that number, but most were green and half had no guns. Shelby's men made the first charge and halted the Union advance. Shelby had been given command of three times the number of men that his rank entitled him to, and he made good use of them. As Sigel's trained German-American troops pummeled the advancing bulk of the rebel infantry, Shelby worked his way through some woods around the Union left. Soon he had flanked the Yankees and was moving around to their rear to threaten their baggage train. The Union artillery exhausted their ammunition trying to shoot down the fast-moving riders. Sigel, finding himself in a perilous position when minutes before he looked ready to win the battle, ordered a retreat. Shelby harassed him for a few miles, dismounting his men to fire at the bluecoats from behind trees.

The battle of Carthage began Shelby's reputation as a cavalry commander, a reputation that would only grow as the war continued. As Price gathered and trained his men at Cowskin Prairie in the southwestern corner of the state, Shelby took his company of Lafayette County Cavalry, now grown to 100 men, on a recruiting mission halfway across the state back to Waverly. It was his first wartime raid. With the countryside full of Union troops, he couldn't stop for long and didn't get many recruits, but he discovered an innate talent for hit-and-run fighting and subterfuge. Union troops wasted many a long day riding around the countryside trying to find Shelby. Central Missouri's thick woodland, filled with underbrush that at times reduces visibility to only a few yards, favors small, guerrilla-style actions. At one point Shelby painted a log black, set it up on the banks of Missouri River like a cannon, and got the steamboat *Sunshine* to pull over and surrender. On it were 1,500 sacks of flour destined for Federal troops in Kansas. Shelby's men took what they needed and distributed the rest to the secessionist residents of Waverly.

Soon Shelby returned to Price's army, which was marching towards the important southwest Missouri town of Springfield with the intention of taking it. Lyon anticipated this and attacked the Confederate camp by surprise early at Wilson's Creek on the morning of August 10, 1861. Despite having 5,400 men to Price's 11,000, Lyon ordered a pincer movement. Sigel attacked from the south but his lines were quickly shattered. Lyon, on the other hand, was well positioned atop a thickly wooded hill to the north with a commanding view of the camp. Shelby tried to charge up the slopes with his cavalry, but found the going too rough and was repulsed with heavy

While J.O. Shelby wasn't present at the battle of Pea Ridge on March 6–8, 1862, it affected him and the entire Confederate cause. The loss made the Confederate high command give up trying to retake Missouri. It transferred the Missouri State Guard and other troops to the East, Shelby's command included. Shelby would not stay in the East for long, as he was dedicated to liberating Missouri. (LoC)

BrigGen Albert Pike, seen here in 1877 wearing Masonic regalia, rode around the Indian Territory in 1861 forming treaties with the Creeks, Chickasaws, Choctaws, Seminoles, Cherokees, and several smaller tribes. He formed an Indian Brigade that fought in several major engagements. The uniforms sent to Pike's brigade were stolen by Shelby's men. (LoC)

casualties. Rebel infantry regiments charged up the hill, which soon became known as "Bloody Hill" during an all-day, vicious seesaw battle in which neither side gained an advantage until Lyon himself was killed and the Union army retreated. The battle was the greatest victory for the Confederacy west of the Mississippi River and taught Shelby a valuable lesson. His men had attacked without artillery support and got mauled. From then on Shelby tried not to make a charge without the aid of artillery. He would bring cannon along on all of his raids.

Price marched all the way to the Missouri River, capturing Lexington and its garrison. Meanwhile, Shelby rode back to Lafayette County on another recruiting mission. He harassed Union detachments and received a hero's welcome in Waverly. Although Price had won a significant victory at Lexington, capturing 3,500 Union troops and all their equipment, he had stretched his supply lines too thin. With Union forces gathering in St. Louis and Kansas City, he had to withdraw to southwest Missouri once again. Shelby rejoined the main column. Winter was setting in and there would be no more major fighting that year. Shelby, however, launched another raid deep behind enemy lines, recruiting more men and keeping the Civil War alive in Union-occupied Missouri. He was rapidly building up a reputation as a tireless fighter for the South.

That winter in camp, the Iron Brigade received their first and only issue of uniforms, and acquired them illegally. In Price's camp was BrigGen Albert Pike, commander of the Confederate Indian brigades. He had ordered 13,000 uniforms for his men, and when the first shipment arrived they were immediately snatched up by Price's white soldiers, Shelby's men included.

This episode was overshadowed in March 1862 when a Union force invaded Arkansas, prompting the battle of Pea Ridge on the 6–8th of that month. In a bloody slugfest, the Confederates were soundly beaten and northwest Arkansas lay open to the Union. Shelby fought well at that battle, but it wasn't enough to change the outcome. After this, the Confederacy west of the river became a slowly fading dream. With the fall of Vicksburg on July 4, 1863, the western Confederacy was cut off from the East. Little Rock, the state capital of Arkansas, fell on September 10. By then the majority of Southern fighting men had crossed the Mississippi to fight in the East, Price included. Shelby, now a colonel, went with his horsemen, now officially the 5th Missouri Confederate Cavalry. It wasn't long before he managed to get his men back where they felt they belonged – in Arkansas, fighting for the liberation of Missouri.

And there Shelby stayed. As the Southern cause faded in the West, his star grew brighter by comparison.

ORIGINS

In formulating the raid for which he is most famous, Shelby had a great deal of experience from which to draw. He had launched numerous small raids himself, both in Bleeding Kansas and during the war proper, and had participated in two major raids under the command of BrigGen John Sappington Marmaduke. The first took place from December 31, 1862, to January 25, 1863, and was meant to take pressure off Confederate forces in Arkansas after another rebel defeat at Prairie Grove on December 7. The commander of the Trans-Mississippi Department, MajGen Thomas Hindman, ordered Marmaduke to take 2,695 men and four cannons on a raid to the north and east of Springfield to cut off the Union supply line and keep the Union army, who had a foothold in the Arkansas River valley, from advancing on Little Rock.

Marmaduke headed out on the last day of the year with the 1,600 troopers of Col Shelby's division among his men. He divided his command into separate sections, making it easier to forage in an area picked almost clean by both armies. Also, having multiple units entering Missouri would hopefully confuse the Union army.

At first all went well. The large force gobbled up Union patrols and a band of lawless bushwhackers, and the artillery they brought along made short work of a Union blockhouse. The commander of another blockhouse burned his fortifications and fled before receiving similar treatment. The raiders also torched several bridges.

Then Marmaduke changed his plans. He had heard Springfield was poorly garrisoned. As the supply depot for all Union forces in the region, it offered a tempting prize. Separated from the railhead at Rolla by 120 miles, it stood isolated in a rough and predominantly pro-Southern land. Marmaduke decided to go beyond Hindman's orders and take the town.

BrigGen John Sappington Marmaduke was Shelby's commander for much of the war and led two raids into Missouri. They met with only limited success and Shelby learned from Marmaduke's mistakes. Despite his failings as a tactician, Shelby respected Marmaduke because he was willing to fight. (LoC)

Ride Around Missouri – Shelby's Great Raid 1863

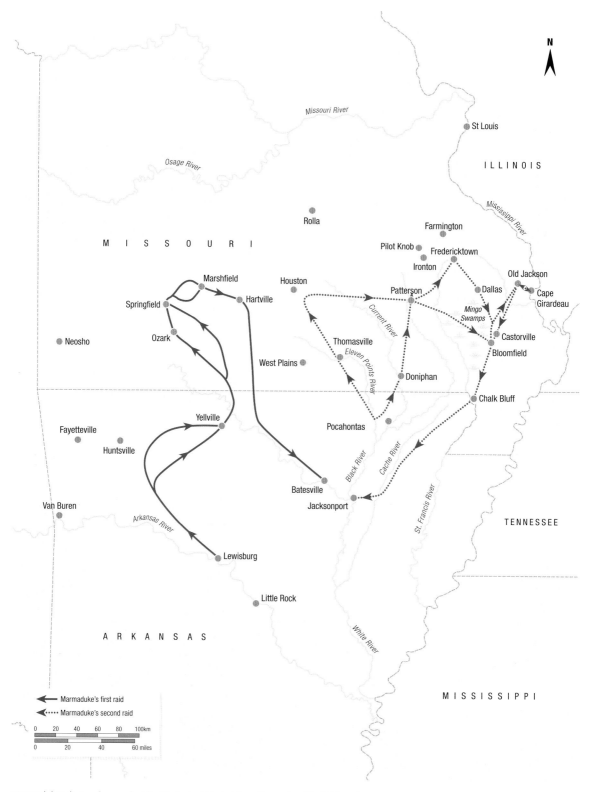

Marmaduke's first and second raids. His first raid lasted from December 31, 1862, to January 25, 1863. His second raid lasted from April 17 to May 2, 1863.

Springfield wasn't as weakly defended as Marmaduke had heard, but its defenses weren't strong either. Five earthwork forts had been planned as a protective ring around the town, but only two were complete enough to be defensible. As soon as Union officer BrigGen Egbert Brown heard of Marmaduke's advance, he set to work strengthening them and blocking off the streets leading to the center of town. Brown was able to draw upon a total of 2,099 men, many of them local militia or civilian volunteers, plus a "Quinine Brigade" of 300 soldiers pulled from the local hospital. He had five pieces of artillery, three of which were old relics that his men hastily mounted on converted wagons.

Marmaduke attacked on January 8. In bitter street-to-street fighting, his men pushed into town but couldn't take the two forts. Every attack on the entrenched positions led to heavy losses. The fighting wavered back and forth for the entire day as Brown sent pleas for help to St. Louis over the telegraph lines, which Marmaduke had failed to cut. By the evening the town was still in Union hands, but the two forces had become so entangled that firing didn't stop until almost midnight.

Shelby urged Marmaduke to pull out and head to the Missouri River. The next morning Marmaduke agreed. One section of his force under Col Porter numbering 825 men had not arrived, and he thought a counterattack late in the day's fighting had been carried out by the vanguard of a Union relief force. Marmaduke also feared the Army of the Frontier might cut off his rear by advancing out of Kansas. The battle of Springfield had cost the Confederates 70–80 killed, 12 captured, and 200 wounded. The Union defenders lost 30 killed, six missing, and 195 wounded. BrigGen Brown had been wounded in the shoulder by a civilian sniper, further proof that while the Union army might control Missouri, there were secessionists everywhere. This sort of incident was commonplace and led to an atmosphere of mistrust between the army and the civilian populace that often led to tragic consequences.

Marmaduke headed east to Hartville in order to rendezvous with Porter, who had already forced the local garrison to surrender without firing a shot and had torched their blockhouse. At 0200hrs on January 11, Porter's command, then numbering 700 after 125 returned home because their unshod horses had become lame, was attacked by a Union force of 700 men and two guns coming to relieve Springfield. The two sides skirmished in the darkness until Marmaduke's main force appeared just before dawn, at which point both sides headed for Hartville in order to take control of the town. The Union force got there first and set up west of town on the brow of a row of low hills. Shelby's men circled them and came into town from the east

Samuel Curtis led the Union to victory at the battle of Pea Ridge on March 6–8, 1862, ending any serious Confederate threat to Missouri and opening up Arkansas to invasion. He was promoted to major-general for that victory and went on to take the Mississippi River port of Helena, Arkansas. His strongly abolitionist views got him reassigned to Kansas and the Indian Territory, which was considered even more of a backwater than Missouri. His son, Maj Henry Z. Curtis, was BrigGen Blunt's adjutant and was killed at the Baxter Springs massacre. Quantrill mistook his body for Blunt's. (LoC)

with the rest of the rebel force soon following. After an artillery duel across Hartville, Shelby learned from scouts that the town lay abandoned and the Federals were in full retreat.

The first part of this intelligence was true, but the second wasn't. Shelby rushed forward even though the area hadn't been properly scouted. When his men came to a fence and started dismantling it, they were surprised by the sudden volley of 700 rifles. Porter fell mortally wounded. Shelby's horse was shot from under him and a bullet struck the star-shaped ornament on his hat, momentarily stunning him. Several times the rebels charged the Union position and were pushed back. Shelby had a second horse shot from under him, but kept up the pressure. Eventually the Union troops ran out of ammunition for their cannons and decided to withdraw. The Union loss at the battle of Hartville was seven killed, 64 wounded, and five taken prisoner, and two missing. The Confederates reported 12 dead, 96 wounded, and three missing, but many historians feel this figure is low.

This battle ended the raid. Union forces were closing in, the element of surprise was long gone, and the rebels had suffered heavy losses. Marmaduke led his men south on a cold, hungry retreat. One cannon was abandoned when its carriage broke. Two hundred mounts became so exhausted that they had to be left behind, leaving their riders to walk back to Arkansas or drop out of the march.

A refugee family arriving in St. Louis. Raids, personal vendettas, and guerrilla attacks made many people flee to the safety of larger cities. This migration put a great strain on Union resources. The depopulation of rural areas both helped and hindered Confederate irregulars and raiders – fewer people made it easier to pass through a region undetected, but it also meant less material aid and local reconnaissance. (LoC)

While not very successful, the raid was a revelation to both sides. It forced the Army of the Frontier to detach forces to fight Marmaduke instead of concentrating on Arkansas, but more importantly it showed how open Missouri was to a large-scale raid. After this the Union worked hard to build more forts in Springfield and other key points, while Hindman and Marmaduke planned more raids.

The next raid occurred from April 17 to May 2, 1863. Earlier in the year MajGen Kirby Smith had been put in command of all Confederate forces west of the Mississippi. Like his predecessor Hindman, he believed in the efficacy of cavalry raids. Marmaduke suggested a diversion into Missouri to draw off pressure on Vicksburg and Little Rock, which were being threatened by Union troops at Helena, Arkansas, on the Mississippi. The plan was to destroy infrastructure along the route before swinging east to take the Union supply depot at the Mississippi port town of Cape Girardeau.

Marmaduke had a large force this time – 5,086 men and eight guns, two of the latter being Parrot rifles, which were more accurate and longer ranged than conventional smoothbores. Unfortunately, 1,200 of his men had no weapons and 900 had no horses. Marmaduke took them along anyway for fear that they'd desert if left behind – the Confederate army west of the Mississippi already had serious problems with morale. Even without these tagalongs, it was the largest Confederate raid yet in the war.

The force moved in two columns. Shelby's brigade headed northwest into Missouri to make it look like he was striking for the center of the state, thus drawing off Union forces from northern Arkansas and southwestern Missouri. Meanwhile, the main force went straight for the town of Patterson, defended by 600 Union militiamen. Alerted by some skirmishing with Union cavalry, the garrison commander in Patterson set fire to his stores and retreated southeast to Bloomfield. Shelby rejoined the column after making his diversion and moved towards Fredericktown while another column headed for Bloomfield to defeat the 2,000 bluecoats there.

Shelby captured a small militia force at Fredericktown, but the other column became bogged down in the Mingo Swamps. Wasting a whole day extricating their cannon and wagons, the rebels couldn't get to Bloomfield in time to stop the local commander from burning his supplies and withdrawing to Cape Girardeau.

Shelby had more success. Based at Fredericktown, he sent raiders to destroy a bridge and long sections of the St. Louis Railroad. He then reunited with the other column and together they struggled through freezing rains towards Cape Girardeau. The town was well defended by the Mississippi to the east and a chain of hills to the west protected by four forts well equipped with artillery. Nevertheless, Marmaduke sent Shelby's brigade to harass the forts. While he was only supposed to drive in the pickets and snipe at the earthworks, aggressive Union movements soon embroiled Shelby in a standing battle. The Union side, supported by artillery fire from the forts, soon pushed the rebels back.

During the afternoon Cape Girardeau was reinforced by troops deployed from boats, and it now had about 3,500 defenders. A force of 5,000 Union

African-American soldiers mustered out at Little Rock, Arkansas, in 1866. Escaped slaves from Arkansas and Missouri made up much of the 1st Kansas Colored Volunteers, the first African-American unit of the US Army to see combat, when they defeated a band of bushwhackers at Island Mound, Missouri, on October 29, 1862. Confederates usually killed black men captured in uniform, and Shelby's raiders were no exception to this rule. Despite this, an estimated 15,000 Arkansas and Missouri blacks fought for their freedom in the Civil War. (LoC)

cavalry was riding in from Fredericktown, which prompted the rebels to withdraw south. The Union forces gave chase and surprised the rebels as they camped for the night. Many units were routed, and if it weren't for a stiff rearguard action by Shelby's men the entire force might have been scattered.

Retreating south, the rebels crossed White Water Bridge and destroyed it behind them, buying some time. They then spent two days making a shaky bridge across the St. Francis River at Chalk Bluff. For eight hours, a thin gray line moved across the trembling construction as other units fought entrenched in a semicircle to keep the Union troops at bay. One by one rebel units crossed the bridge, the semicircle tightening until the last man crossed to the south bank and the rebels cut the bridge's moorings.

The Union force could never catch up now, but the raiders had to struggle through the swamps south of the river for three days. They made it back to Jacksonport, Arkansas, without further incident, having lost 30 killed, 60 wounded, and 120 missing, while recruiting 150 men in Missouri. The large number of missing suggests that Marmaduke's fears of desertion were well founded.

Marmaduke's poor planning had made the raid a failure. Slowed by a large wagon train, he couldn't move rapidly enough to catch isolated Union garrisons unawares. Poor reconnaissance meant he often led his men onto bad roads or into nearly impenetrable swamps. He also hadn't worked out his retreat, an essential part of any plan for a raid. The rains made the St. Francis rise out of its banks, and if it weren't for the efforts of his amateur engineers his entire force might have been captured. In the end, only a small amount of infrastructure had been destroyed, the Union armies hadn't moved from their positions threatening Little Rock, and Cape Girardeau remained intact.

In the summer of 1863, Shelby again took part in a major operation. LtGen Theophilus Holmes, commander of Confederate forces in Arkansas, decided to attack Helena on the Mississippi River. Helena was a Union foothold in eastern Arkansas and an important staging point for Ulysses Grant's operations against Vicksburg. If the rebels could take Helena, it would severely hamper the siege of Vicksburg. Helena was guarded by only 4,100 Union troops, but heavily protected by concentric rings of rifle pits and five forts bristling with cannon. Holmes led the forces of generals Price, Marmaduke, James Fagan, and Lucius Walker. Shelby rode with Price's outfit. In total, the Confederates numbered about 7,600. Standard military theory dictates that to take a fortified position it's best to have a three-to-one superiority in numbers; the rebels had slightly less than two-to-one. Nevertheless they prepared to attack Helena at daylight on July 4.

MajGen Benjamin Prentiss, the Union commander at Helena, heard of the rebel advance. His men were up and ready well before dawn, and all the roads approaching town had been blocked. Fagan reported that "the road was completely filled with felled timber, the largest forest growth intermingling and overlapping its whole length, while on either side precipitous and impassable ravines were found running up to the very entrenchments of the enemy." The blockage ran for miles, and with daylight fast approaching there was no time to clear it out. Men had to crawl on all fours or hop over giant trunks in order to proceed. All the commanders except Shelby left their artillery behind. Shelby's men did what they usually did. If they needed to get artillery where horses couldn't go, they carried the artillery.

Price personally led a spirited attack on the Union center, while Marmaduke, Shelby, and Walker came up on the Union right. Marmaduke attacked, but found himself surrounded on three sides. Walker declined to aid him because, he said, that would expose himself to being flanked and would open a gap through which the Federals could completely encircle Marmaduke. Shelby was busy in an artillery duel with the forts and the Union gunboat USS *Tyler*. He requested permission to advance, but never received it. Holmes, always an indecisive commander, couldn't figure out what to do and only gave vague orders. While Price managed to take several Union positions, he found himself enfiladed and had to withdraw. Shelby also came under heavy fire and was shot in the arm, the bullet entering his wrist and ranging up the arm before exiting near the elbow.

By 1030hrs it was all over. Holmes ordered a retreat. Weeping, he told Marmaduke that the Army of the Trans-Mississippi was now, "an army of prisoners, and self-supporting at that." Prentiss thought the rebels were regrouping for another attack and so didn't give chase. Later he went out and counted the Confederate losses and realized no attack would have come – 1,636 rebels were dead, wounded, or missing, compared with only 206 Union casualties. Shelby spent several weeks bedridden in the care of a doctor.

INITIAL STRATEGY

Now that the Union had secured Helena and northwestern Arkansas, they were finally able to realize their plans of marching on Little Rock. As the Union troops closed in on the Arkansas state capital, bad blood between Marmaduke and Walker over the battle of Helena flared into a duel. Marmaduke shot Walker dead. The general was briefly detained, but good commanders were in such short supply in the Trans-Mississippi that he soon received a pardon. The city fell on September 10, 1863.

By the autumn of 1863 the Confederacy was in serious trouble. Robert E. Lee's Army of Northern Virginia had been badly mauled at Gettysburg that summer, and the Mississippi River stronghold of Vicksburg had fallen the same day that the attack on Helena failed. The Mississippi was now a Union river and the Confederacy had been cut in half. With the fall of Little Rock, Price's rebel army withdrew 65 miles southwest to Arkadelphia. Other than minor cavalry raids and actions by countless guerrillas, many of whom acted more like bandits than Confederate irregulars, there was no significant rebel presence in Missouri or northern Arkansas. The Confederate troops clustered in southern Arkansas, Louisiana, and Texas were poorly armed, poorly fed, worn out by a seemingly endless series of reverses, and deserting in large numbers.

Kirby Smith, however, remained convinced that the Trans-Mississippi theater could still play an important role in the war. He wanted to contribute more to the war effort than a simple holding action against Union troops along the Arkansas River and the occasional temporary harassment deeper into Union-held territory. Yet he wasn't sure how. His army, although it numbered 67,000 men on paper, wasn't nearly so large in reality. Men were scattered in garrisons from the Mississippi to Mexico. On the Mississippi, on the White River, and on the shores of Louisiana and Texas, they spied on Union gunboats and guarded against troop landings. Men were needed along the Mexican border to stop bandits from coming north and to guard the wagon trains bringing priceless supplies from the outside world, the only route not subject to Union blockade. Men were needed in north and west

SEPTEMBER 21 1863

Shelby receives final permission from Price to raid Missouri

JOHN NEWMAN EDWARDS

The story of J.O. Shelby and his Iron Brigade cannot be told without discussing the writer John Newman Edwards, because Edwards was in large part responsible for creating Shelby's legend. Edwards was one of Shelby's oldest friends. Shelby always had a kind word to say about Edwards, and Edwards simply idolized Shelby.

Born in Virginia in 1839, Edwards moved to Lexington, Missouri, in the 1850s, where he soon got caught up in Bleeding Kansas. A devout states-rights man, he espoused the Southern view in a series of increasingly fiery articles as editor of the *Lexington Expositor*. Edwards was a flamboyant writer even by the flowery standards of the day. To him all Yankees were the vilest villains, and all Southerners were bold champions of society and civilization. During these tumultuous times he met J.O. Shelby and the two became fast friends. They hunted together, raided Kansas together, and Edwards even helped plan Shelby's wedding in 1858.

Edwards was no armchair soldier like so many newspapermen then and now. He rode with the Iron Brigade right from the beginning and fought in every battle and skirmish. Veterans of the elite unit always noted that Edwards was one of the bravest of the brave. His ability earned him the rank of major by the fall of 1862. During the 1863 attack on Cape Girardeau, a shell fragment tore away part of the inside of his leg and he was captured and made prisoner, but was exchanged shortly thereafter. His battlefield accomplishments, however, paled in comparison to the service he did the Iron Brigade as their chief propagandist. He became Shelby's adjutant shortly after being promoted and began writing Shelby's official reports. Gone was Shelby's spare prose, and in came grandiose hyperbole that made every Missouri farm boy on a horse look like a Knight of the Round Table. Shelby was their King Arthur, leading them through a series of exaggerated encounters against huge Federal armies. It would be interesting to know what Shelby's superiors thought of these reports. As records of what actually happened they leave much to be desired, but they do make great reading, and perhaps Sterling Price and Kirby Smith didn't mind a bit of literary embellishment after wading through reams of dreary memoranda.

While Edwards' contributions to the *Official Records* are unreliable, they are often the only records we have of

smaller skirmishes. Even Iron Brigade veterans laughed at some of his exaggerations, but always said his dates and general information were correct. Another journalist, George Creel, used to visit Shelby long after the war and wrote: "When I dropped in to see the General, it was usually an hour before I could get away. As a rule, members of his old command sat with him, and when dispute occurred as to a date or incident, they turned to their Bible, Major John N. Edwards' chronicle of the expedition." In a letter to Shelby biographer Daniel O'Flaherty, Creel said, "Major Edwards never failed to gild the lily, but for what Colonel Elliott and others told me ... he usually had a basis of fact."

After the war, Edwards wrote two books about the Iron Brigade: *Shelby and His Men; or, The War in the West* (1867), and *Shelby's Expedition to Mexico: An Unwritten Leaf of the War* (1872). The latter is the only full record of that expedition. Edwards was also responsible for the fame of bushwhackers such as William Quantrill and "Bloody Bill" Anderson. His *Noted Guerrillas; or, The Warfare on the Border* (1875) raised the bushwhackers to the status of avenging angels. All three books are amusing reads, but should be taken with two grains of salt and several other sources.

Edwards' most lasting legacy was his launching to fame of two other guerrillas – Frank and Jesse James. As editor of the *Kansas City Times* during the James gang's postwar crime spree, he wrote gushing editorials that portrayed the James brothers as victims of Yankee oppression. It was a story many embittered ex-rebels wanted to hear, and the James legend was born. After Jesse was assassinated, Edwards acted as a mediator between Frank and Missouri governor Thomas Crittenden, a former colonel of the 7th Missouri State Militia Cavalry. Bushwhacker and bluecoat came face to face in a highly publicized meeting at the capitol office in Jefferson City on October 5, 1882. Frank gave a flowery speech and surrendered his guns. The meeting had the Edwards touch, a brilliant bit of public relations that ensured the endurance of the James legend and helped get Frank acquitted of all charges.

John Newman Edwards died in 1889, but his legacy has lived on by creating a legend of the Civil War, and the greatest figure of the Wild West.

Civilians receiving travel passes from Federal officials in St. Louis. As guerrilla attacks rose, daily life became harder and harder for secessionist civilians, increasing their bitterness. Shelby hoped his raid would tap into this anger and attract volunteers to his colors, but by late 1863 most true rebels had already joined up. (LoC)

Texas to discourage Indian raids. Men were needed in the interiors of the states to fight Unionist guerrillas and bands of roaming deserters turned outlaw. Men were needed to hold the line against MajGen Frederick Steele's troops along the Arkansas River. Men were needed to hunt down the men who went AWOL.

Smith was left with relatively few troops actually available and prepared to go into battle, and these had suffered so many defeats he may have lost his faith in them, or at least in many of their commanders. A plague of caution had spread through the Trans-Mississippi command. Smith was one of the least affected, but he didn't know how he could strike against the Yankees.

J.O. Shelby showed him how. Shelby agitated for another raid into Missouri. This time he wanted to lead it himself. He had learned from Marmaduke's successes and mistakes and felt he could do better. He saw that isolated Union garrisons were vulnerable to swift attacks, but he also saw that larger enemy forces could put up a determined resistance. Shelby realized the futility of attacking sizeable fortifications such as Springfield and the danger of getting embroiled in large-scale battles. Also, he realized Marmaduke had blundered badly by bringing along a large wagon train and many unarmed men, who only slowed the column down. Shelby's force would be smaller and leaner, with a better knowledge of the terrain so as not to repeat the fiasco of getting caught in a swamp.

But convincing Price and Holmes and Kirby Smith that a colonel could succeed where a brigadier-general had failed was going to be difficult.

Circumstances had changed. Instead of starting out from north of the Arkansas River, with a firmly held state of Arkansas at his back, Shelby would have to start from southwestern Arkansas, cross the river undetected by the cordon of Union troops, thrust deep into enemy territory, extricate himself from Missouri, and then sneak back across the river while avoiding what would surely be a fully alerted defense. To make matters worse, Shelby still suffered acutely from the wound he'd received at Helena. The chance of disaster was high, and the last thing the Confederacy needed was another fiasco. It's a testament to Shelby's skill and his personal charisma that his superiors gave it even a passing thought, let alone their approval.

Shelby first went to the man whom he knew would be most likely to listen to his case: Missouri Confederate governor-in-exile Thomas Reynolds. Governor Jackson had died the previous year and Reynolds was now in charge of a state he couldn't visit. Shelby told him of grand plans to stoke the fires of rebellion in Missouri and threaten the state capital itself. Reynolds' eyes must have gleamed

MajGen Kirby Smith took over the Confederate Department of the Trans-Mississippi in March 1863. Despite his having a large number of men at his disposal, they were spread out defending a huge area and he lacked the manpower to launch any serious offensives. He relied on guerrillas and cavalry raiders to keep the war alive in the West. (LoC)

at the thought. The governor went to Smith and Price and managed to convince them. Shelby also had to gain the approval of Marmaduke, the commander of Confederate cavalry in Arkansas. Marmaduke had his doubts, pointing out that Shelby may not be capable of enduring a long raid in his injured condition. Shelby scoffed that he "would rather go and lose both hands than remain idle in Arkansas."

Shelby treated Gen Holmes even more dismissively. After Helena, Holmes had become morose and irritable. Before Shelby set out on his raid, Holmes ordered him to a meeting. As soon as he entered the room, an eyewitness reported that Holmes snapped, "Sir, your men are nothing but a set of thieves, and their thieving must be stopped."

"Sir, whoever told you that, lies," Shelby replied coolly.

"I believe it is true," Holmes said.

"Why?" Shelby asked.

"Because everybody says so," Holmes replied.

"Do you believe a thing when everybody says it?"

"I certainly do."

"Do you know what everybody says about you?" Shelby asked.

"No, sir, I do not!"

"They say you are a damned old fool," Shelby stated, then turned and walked out.

Shelby had Reynolds on his side, and he had permission to ride. To him that was all that mattered.

THE PLAN

Shelby's intentions were threefold. First, he wanted to cause enough trouble in Missouri that troops there wouldn't be able to help MajGen William Rosecrans at Chattanooga, Tennessee, where Rosecrans was locked in a bloody struggle with Confederate general Braxton Bragg. There had been urgent calls for reinforcements from the Union high command, but the commander of the Department of Missouri, MajGen John Schofield, had so far been resisting, stating he needed all his men to hold the Arkansas River line and deal with the countless guerrillas in Missouri and Arkansas. (Despite its name, the Department of Missouri also included Arkansas.) Shelby wanted to help Schofield keep Union troops tied up in Missouri and along the Arkansas River. Even if Schofield didn't cooperate, even if he drained Missouri of men to help the situation in Tennessee, this could be good for Shelby too, because then he might be able to take Jefferson City. Capturing the state capital, even if only for a day or two, would be a major coup.

Second, Shelby wanted to raise recruits. He was an extremely popular commander, especially in the secessionist western Missouri River counties of "Little Dixie," and he hoped to bolster Price's undermanned regiments. Previous recruiting raids had met with modest success. With life getting ever harder for Southern sympathizers in Missouri, Shelby may have thought he'd get more recruits than ever.

Third, by causing as much damage to Union infrastructure as possible, he wanted to keep the war in Missouri. By off-footing the Union, they'd be less likely to launch another offensive into Arkansas, and a strong rebel showing in Missouri would help keep the flame of rebellion lit in what had been an occupied state for more than a year. Edwards said that Shelby intended to "keep alive in the hearts of his friends that spirit of opposition and hatred of Federal rule worthy to be ranked among the best virtues of the human heart."

Shelby had a tough job ahead of him. First he had to move 65 miles from Arkadelphia to the Arkansas River without alerting Union patrols. The region was rife with guerrillas and Confederate patrols, and the Union troops tended to keep to their well-guarded garrisons along the river. When they

SEPTEMBER 22 1863

Shelby leaves Arkadelphia, Arkansas

MajGen John Schofield, commander of the Department of Missouri, had trouble figuring out Shelby's movements from his base in St. Louis. Time and again he misjudged Shelby's intentions, while some of his subordinates in the field guessed correctly and gave chase. (LoC)

ventured out, it was generally in large groups that Shelby's swift-moving riders could easily avoid. The Union troops rarely patrolled very far to the south in any case, preferring to guard the river.

Next he had to cross the Arkansas River undetected. At this time of year the river ran low and was fordable in many spots, but there were some 30,000 Union troops under MajGen Steele in the Arkansas River valley. Most were garrisoned in Little Rock and Van Buren, with smaller garrisons spread out at regular intervals along the river. These troops were content to hold the river and maintain a frontline against any major Confederate offensive. With the river in its low season, patrols were even fewer than normal since there was no shipping to protect, and the troops mainly stayed in their forts, assuming there'd be no major operations until the following spring.

Blockhouses varied widely in construction, from little more than log cabins with loopholes to complex miniature fortresses. Even basic ones like this two-story structure were effective at stopping guerrillas, and were built across Union-held Missouri and northern Arkansas to guard towns, bridges, and railroads. In some Missouri towns, brick courthouses in the middle of large town squares offered a ready-made defense that only required sandbags in the windows. Shelby knew he'd be facing many blockhouses and fortified buildings and therefore brought along artillery. (LoC)

Once across, Shelby and his men would have to head north through the rest of Arkansas and the Boston Mountains into Missouri. This region was only lightly garrisoned and rarely patrolled by Union troops. It was filled with guerrillas, bandits, and deserters, and the Union had pretty much given up trying to control it. While the lawlessness meant misery for the few civilians still clinging to their farms, Steele felt it had no strategic value. Shelby would be reasonably safe in this region, but would have to move fast because even here there were people who might alert the Union commanders to his presence.

Next came the hard part. In Missouri there were 60,000 Federal troops and 50,000 militia under Schofield, who was based in St. Louis. The Federal troops were mostly in the main cities or in the southern and southwestern parts of the state hunting guerrillas, as well as in eastern Kansas, which was also part of Schofield's command. The militia was spread out over all the state, guarding their local areas. They were of two varieties. The Enrolled Missouri Militia, founded in 1862 to reduce the number of Federal troops needed in the state, was made up of every able-bodied man and included many individuals of doubtful quality. Some were even Confederate deserters who had taken an oath of loyalty. They didn't have uniforms, were indifferently trained, and were only called up during times of immediate danger to their local area. Still, some Enrolled Missouri Militia regiments had shown pluck on the battlefield. More capable was the Provisional

Enrolled Missouri Militia, created in February 1863 and made up of the best men drawn from the Enrolled Missouri Militia. They served longer terms of duty, had better training, were provided with uniforms, and served under Schofield's direct command. Only true Union men who showed valor in the field could get into this militia. One would think that men of this description would already be in the Federal army, but such was the state of lawlessness in Missouri, with guerrillas terrorizing the countryside and neighbors taking out vendettas against one another, that many men preferred to stay close to home in order to protect their families and property. The troops of the Provisional Enrolled Missouri Militia had no shortage of fighting to do. The 11 regiments of this outfit were mostly in western, southwestern, and central Missouri, especially the Little Dixie hotbed of secessionism. These were the very places where Shelby planned to do his recruiting.

Shelby hoped to get into Missouri before being detected or at least before meeting significant resistance. The southernmost counties would be relatively easy. Like northern Arkansas, they were sparsely populated even in peacetime and were now mostly abandoned. Union garrisons were more numerous here than in northern Arkansas. These posed a problem, but might offer Shelby some easy early victories. Most garrisons were isolated blockhouses or fortified brick buildings, often courthouses in town squares. The detachments rarely numbered more than a few hundred men, and often considerably fewer. They could stand against bands of guerrillas, but wouldn't last long against an elite force of soldiers supplied with artillery. Shelby's goal was the Missouri heartland, however, and he wouldn't attack these little forts unless he'd already lost the element of surprise.

Central Missouri was the real prize, and the real trouble. Shelby had no illusions of making it this far without Schofield being on alert. The militia would be armed and ready, Federal troops would be on the move, and Union cavalry would be closing in from all sides. Shelby would need to rely on the hard fighting and even harder riding that his men had proven themselves capable of so many times before. He'd ride through central Missouri, now more than 400 miles from his base in Arkadelphia, and hit the Union troops there with more force than they'd felt since Price's retreat from Lexington back in 1862.

Shelby didn't designate a strict route of march or specific targets. He didn't make detailed plans. As Edwards put it, "Preparations for raids to Missouri were never long in the making, and this one grew as swiftly as a young man's love." This action would be a raid of opportunity, striking at the spots that offered the most reward for the least risk. There would be none of Marmaduke's sieges or set-piece battles. Shelby's men would move in, wreck havoc, rally as many recruits as possible, and get out fast.

Like many cavalry raiders, Shelby had a few tricks to increase his speed and shake off pursuit. One was to feed his horses on the march. The men would gather up bundles of grain from fields or barns on the way, and each man would hold one behind him so the horse next in file could munch on the move. Fatigue of men and horses was a critical problem on a raid, especially ones that went deep into enemy territory without hope of support, like

Shelby's. He'd give his men brief rests when he could, usually at night, and then set out before sunrise. He also tried to rest his horses on the march by rotating those who took the advance guards. Elliot's scouts usually ranged ahead, but for his regular advance guard he rotated one-third of his men for the duty. Thus a third would go on ahead, then rest as the main body came up, then that third would be replaced by another third. This pattern allowed for short rests for whomever was in the advanced guard.

The retreat would be the toughest challenge. By that stage all of Missouri would be on the march, Gen Steele would be waiting for him along the Arkansas, and the retreat would be one of constant riding and fighting until they made it back home. This danger, however, was actually one of the major goals of the raid – the more Shelby could stir things up, the more soldiers would be chasing him rather than marching against Bragg in Tennessee.

The Men

Shelby handpicked 750 men: 200 under Capt David Gordon, 200 under Maj David Shanks, 200 under LtCol James Hooper, 100 scouts from Maj Ben Elliot's command, and 50 scouts under Capt "Tuck" Thorpe. Shelby only picked longtime veterans who had proven their worth in previous raids. There'd be no shanghaied deserters like those Marmaduke burdened himself with. Because of the state of some of his horses, the quality of a man's mount was also a factor in whether or not he was picked. Most of the men were young, in their early twenties. For artillery he had two pieces under Lt David Harris – a brass 6-pdr smoothbore and a 10-pdr Parrot rifle. Both had been captured from the enemy.

The reenactment group Shelby's 5th Missouri Cavalry overruns Union troops. Note the variety of clothing among the raiders, from Federal uniforms to civilian garb. The loose formation in the charge is also accurate. (From the collection of Scott Hughes)

PREVIOUS PAGE: Shelby's raiders rode light in order to move and strike quickly. Here we see a typical raider and his equipment. Most noticeable is the fact that his uniform is more Union than Confederate. While being captured in the wrong uniform usually meant facing a firing squad, Shelby's men liked the camouflage Union uniforms provided. This raider wears a Union jacket, belt, belt buckle, and cartridge bag. He has Confederate pants, a slouch hat with a sprig of red sumac to identify him as a rebel, and high riding boots. Shelby's men carried a variety of weapons. Most had at least one Colt Navy revolver, the favored weapon of cavalry raiders for its rate of fire and ease of handling on horseback. When fighting on foot, something Shelby's men did frequently, they used Enfield or Springfield rifled muskets. The preferred weapon was the Sharps rifle which, though uncommon, had a good rate of fire and was highly accurate. In his pockets are two spare revolver cylinders. Reloading was far too time consuming to do in battle, so raiders liked to prepare extra cylinders ahead of time. His horse has a standard Union issue McClellan saddle, yet another item he has taken from a prisoner. In the saddlebags are a meager supply of hardtack and parched corn, a sewing kit, dining set, and boxes of prepared cartridges for his Springfield musket. A bedroll is tied behind.

Elliot's men deserve special mention. They were the elite of an elite force, always in the vanguard, and with an excellent knowledge of Missouri's terrain and back roads. Just as Shelby handpicked every man in his Iron Brigade, Elliot handpicked every man who joined his scouts. All were veterans of the Kansas–Missouri border wars or veteran members of cavalry units. Shelby's men vied with one another to get into Elliot's outfit, considering it a promotion and a mark of honor. Elliot's vanguard usually ended up in the thick of any fight and took the heaviest casualties, ensuring that a steady supply of men would always be getting the honor of joining. The *Official Records* make no mention of Maj Elliot himself coming along on the raid, and it appears his men were commanded by Capt Thorpe.

In addition to the above-mentioned troops, Shelby requested that he be joined by some of the mounted recruiters who sneaked around rural Missouri gathering volunteers. While Shelby's raiders knew Missouri well, the recruiters were more up-to-date on Union dispositions, and which locals to trust and which were Union sympathizers or informants. When raiding deep within enemy territory, such knowledge could mean the difference between success and failure.

The new recruits coming from Missouri would be indifferently armed with whatever they could bring from home or steal from Union soldiers. Some, in fact, were former members of the Enrolled Missouri Militia. As we have seen, they received minimal training and no uniforms, but they did get guns. Even paroled Confederate prisoners and deserters had to join the Enrolled Missouri Militia. Some hardcore rebels couldn't bear the thought of fighting for a Union outfit and ran off to join the guerrillas. Such is what Frank James did. He had been part of Price's army, but fell sick during the retreat from Lexington and was captured and paroled. He went home to his farm and would have probably spent the rest of the war tending crops if the government hadn't forced him to pick sides. Other secessionists made their way to Arkansas to reenlist in the Confederate army. Many Southern-leaning individuals did join the Enrolled Missouri Militia so as to protect their farms from the increasing lawlessness of wartime Missouri. Still others took the guns and ammunition provided, and deserted back to the Confederate side as soon as possible.

While the new recruits would provide local knowledge but mediocre weapons, Shelby's men came armed with the best guns they could steal from the Yankees. The gun of choice was the Sharps rifle, a breech-loading .52-cal rifle famed for its accuracy and ease of reloading. A trained man could get off ten shots a minute. Because it was a breech-loader it could be loaded from a prone position, making it excellent for using from ambush positions. Some of these weapons dated back to Bleeding Kansas, where they had been prised from the cold, dead fingers of Kansas free-staters. There was also a Sharps carbine for cavalry use. A more common rifle was the Springfield rifled musket, the favored infantry weapon of both sides. Some were distributed by the Confederate army, while others were taken from the many garrisons and supply depots the Iron Brigade plundered. Firing a .58-cal Minié ball, it had good stopping power and accuracy and could be fired three times a minute.

Despite being in a cavalry brigade, Shelby's men all carried rifles because they so often fought as dragoons, dismounting to engage the enemy.

The raiders also liked to have one or more .36-cal Colt Navy revolvers, which were considered easier to use on horseback than the slightly heavier .44-cal Colt Army revolver. Revolvers came in handy in cavalry charges or rearguard actions while trying to stave off pursuers. Their high rate of fire was especially useful in close combat.

It is likely that Shelby's raiders also brought along a variety of other weapons. Some may have had the older Enfield .577-cal rifled musket, although these would have been replaced with the better Springfields when the opportunity arose. There were probably a few shotguns and cavalry carbines in the ranks as well, and examples of the many types of pistols of the period.

The most important man in the Iron Brigade was Shelby himself. Young and good-looking with piercing eyes and a thick beard, he cut a fine figure in a black slouch hat with the front pinned back and adorned with a gold buckle. A black feather plume on his hat soon became a trademark. As one Arkansas soldier put it: "He was the finest looking man I ever saw, black hair and handsome features. *He looked like somebody*. He looked like someone who had something to him, like he was a fine strong man, which no doubt he was."

Reenactors from Shelby's 5th Missouri Cavalry form a line to support their artillery. Unlike some cavalry raiders, Shelby made the artillery an integral part of his brigade. (From the collection of Scott Hughes)

THE RAID

Ho Boys! Make a noise;
The Yankees are afraid;
The river's up, Hell's to pay;
Shelby's on a raid!

Setting Out

On September 21, 1863, Shelby received the approval he so desired. General Price authorized him to take the men and two cannons he had chosen and a dozen wagons of ammunition. While these wagons would slow him down somewhat, Shelby didn't want to strike deep into Missouri without artillery support and a large amount of small-arms ammunition. Since any sizeable Union force would be similarly encumbered, and the wagon train was much smaller than that brought along by Marmaduke, Shelby reasoned it wouldn't be too much of an impediment. Wagons could be discarded as supplies were used up, reducing the burden on his forces. He also brought along at least two ambulances to carry the wounded.

Price ordered Cols John Coffee and Dewitt Hunter, two experienced recruiters who each commanded a few hundred cavalry in Missouri, to join Shelby in the southwestern part of the state. Their local knowledge and extra manpower would prove vital. As an added incentive, Price offered Shelby a promotion to brigadier-general if the raid went well. By all rights this honor should have been given to the talented cavalry commander at least a year before, but the older officers in the Confederate high command, many of whom were West Pointers or veterans of the Mexican–American War, were slow to recognize ability in one so young and without formal training.

Shelby's men set out the next day. Elliot's scouts rode ahead wearing full Federal uniforms and carrying an American flag. Many of Shelby's men wore partial or full Union uniforms. To signal to one another that they weren't actually Union troops, the raiders wore a sprig of red sumac on their hats. Shelby didn't need any sumac because the long plume on his slouch hat was

SEPTEMBER 26 1863

Fight with 200 bushwhackers in Ouachita Mountains

30

almost the unofficial flag of the Iron Brigade. The Confederate uniforms they'd stolen from the Indians had worn thin, and with no new uniforms being issued, the men took what they needed from Union prisoners or casualties. Shelby encouraged this practice because it helped fool the enemy. On more than one occasion his men were able to get in close on unsuspecting Union troops and open fire.

This tactic was, of course, against the laws of war. Many bushwhackers did this too, including William Quantrill's and "Bloody Bill" Anderson's notorious killers. The Union command in Missouri issued strict instructions that any rebel caught not wearing a uniform, or wearing a Union uniform, would be shot on the spot. For this reason many Union records refer to Shelby as a "guerrilla" or "partisan ranger." Shelby objected to these labels and on one occasion even wrote to a Union officer in protest.

The Iron Brigade headed for Clarksville, Arkansas, about a hundred miles upstream (west) of Little Rock. Here they hoped to cross the river. They traveled fast to evade detection. On September 26 the vanguard discovered 200 guerrillas near Caddo Gap in the Ouachita Mountains. This was no organized Unionist band like some that plagued Arkansas, nor was it a group of rebel bushwhackers, but a mix of Confederate deserters and Unionist jayhawkers who had become bandits. This was all too common in the Trans-Mississippi. They'd recently killed 20 local men and were the terror of the region. The raiders waited until dark and then launched a surprise attack on their camp, killing 79 and taking 34 prisoners. The rest fled. The captives

SEPTEMBER 27 1863

Fight with the First Federal Arkansas Infantry at Moffat's Station; Shelby crosses Arkansas River

Shelby's 5th Missouri Cavalry, a reenactment group, harasses a Unionist farmhouse. Shelby's men took what they needed from Northerners, but left secessionists alone. (From the collection of Scott Hughes)

were lined up, given a trial, and all but three sentenced to be shot. The leader of the band, a Capt McGinnis, asked to have the chance to pray before meeting his maker. Edwards records his words as: "Oh God! Bless this Union and all its loyal defenders; bless the poor ignorant rebels who persist in hardening their hearts and stiffening their necks; bless Mrs McGinnis and her children; bless the Constitution, which has been wrongly interpreted; and eradicate slavery from the earth."

Despite his eleventh-hour claims to Unionism, it's doubtful McGinnis led a real Union partisan band. The lawlessness in Missouri and Arkansas encouraged many opportunists to prey upon the civilian population. These groups were hated by Union and Confederate commanders alike, and MajGen Steele probably didn't shed any tears for McGinnis and his crew, assuming he even knew they existed. Shelby's scouts encountered several smaller groups of what Edwards refers to as "Federal outlaws and jayhawkers." Like the men under Capt McGinnis, these were fighters of uncertain or no loyalty and these engagements were more about hunting down criminals than engaging with the enemy. Fortunately these groups had little or no contact with regular Union forces, so there was no serious danger of Steele getting to know of Shelby's movements.

But the secrecy wasn't to last. On September 27, Capt "Tuck" Thorpe's scouts came into contact with 50 men of the 1st Arkansas Federal Infantry Regiment at Moffat's Station, only 12 miles from the river. Thorpe's men charged immediately, forcing the bluecoats back to a line of trees. There they held firm and Thorpe's men had to withdraw under heavy fire. Shelby came up with the main column and dismounted two regiments. As these regiments skirmished with the Federals, Shanks' and Gordon's men attacked on both flanks simultaneously. The Union troops retreated, leaving two dead, two wounded, and 28 prisoners. The prisoners were paroled, except for one who turned out to be a Confederate deserter and was executed. Shelby's men also captured three wagons of quartermaster and commissary supplies. The engagement was a quick and easy victory for Shelby, but it contained an element of defeat. Once the remnants of the Union detachment made it back to camp, the whole Arkansas valley would be on alert within hours.

The Iron Brigade galloped to the Arkansas River, fording it as the sun set. Once across they rested for two hours and divided up the captured supplies. Shelby sent out scouts upstream and downstream towards Clarkesville and Dardanelle to check on Union movements there, then performed a night march, not resting until the Mulberry River 15 miles northwest of Ozark. Union pursuit was not forthcoming. Steele didn't send out a major force against Shelby and was apparently unaware that the force that defeated the 1st Arkansas was any major threat.

For the next three days, Shelby made easy marches, conserving strength for the greater exertions ahead. On the night of September 29 they were at Bentonville, which had been recently burned to the ground by Union troops. Shelby's scouts cut the telegraph lines connecting Fayetteville, Arkansas, and St. Louis, Missouri, thereby severing any quick communication between Steele and Schofield. Shelby also sent Col Horace Brand with some men riding through northeastern Arkansas to recruit men to attack Rolla as a diversionary tactic. Rolla was never attacked, and it's unclear what happened to Col Brand. At McKissick's Springs on either September 30 or October 1 (Edwards says "31 September"!), Shelby's men met up with 200 Arkansas and Missouri recruits led by Col DeWitt Hunter.

Union Confusion

The land the Iron Brigade rode through wasn't entirely unoccupied, and the raiders chatted with several farmers along the way. Shelby's men were friendly to those noncombatants who acted friendly to them, but they always included a bit of disinformation in their conversation, knowing word travels fast in rural communities. They told everyone they were going to join up with BrigGen William Cabell and his 1,200 men. This wasn't true, but it soon reached the ears of the Union commander at Fayetteville, Col M. La Rue Harrison. On October 1 he sent Schofield this information and reported Shelby's strength as 1,300 men and three pieces of artillery. His intent, Harrison believed, was to attack Cassville in the extreme southwestern part of Missouri.

The commander at Springfield, Col John Edwards (no relation to Maj John Newman Edwards), ordered all available units in the Cassville area to gather at Cassville itself. He also reinforced Springfield in case Shelby wanted to repeat Marmaduke's attack. Shelby, of course, had no intention of heading northwest to attack either town, but his disinformation helped clear the way for his ride further to the west. On October 2 he rendezvoused with Col John Coffee and his 400 men near Pineville. Coffee was one of the most active Confederate recruiters in the state, and an experienced officer, having served with the US Cavalry before the war. With Coffee's reinforcements, Shelby now officially had 1,350 men. He might have had slightly more as individual recruits and, according to some sources, guerrilla bands joined him as well.

The next day Shelby bypassed Cassville, giving it a wide berth of more than 50 miles. While Cassville was now strongly protected, the town north of it, Neosho, was guarded by only 300 men. Neosho was the largest Union supply depot in the region. Shelby's riders quickly enveloped the town on October 4. At first the outnumbered garrison fought hard and drove the rebels out of town before retreating into the fortified courthouse. Firing continued for an hour until Shelby decided to save time and men by rolling up his artillery and sending a couple of rounds through the walls. This convinced the defenders to surrender. They were disarmed, paroled, and released. The Union officer in charge says two Union soldiers were killed, two wounded, and that two more were murdered by Coffee's men after they surrendered. He also claims five Confederates were killed and nine wounded.

Neosho was a rich prize. The garrison had 400 horses, medical supplies, ammunition, and hundreds of Colt Navy revolvers and Sharps carbines. There were also plenty of uniforms, and soon most if not all of his command wore blue.

Shelby's men had ridden hard nearly all day and had fought a skirmish at Neosho, yet Shelby wasn't content. He pushed his men another 20 miles

SEPTEMBER 29
1863

Iron Brigade
reaches
Bentonville,
Arkansas

northeast to Sarcoxie, only letting them rest for five hours along the way. This was typical of the raider's hard-riding style.

Much of the region had been destroyed by the war. Edwards describes how at Sarcoxie "bare and fire-scarred chimneys point with skeleton fingers to heaven for vengeance." For the next two days the raiders continued their hard ride north, stopping to burn Bower's Mill, a gathering place for local militia, or as Edwards put it, "a notorious pest spot ... which was sacked and swept from the earth, to pollute it no more forever." During this time Schofield sent a telegram to BrigGen Thomas Ewing, commander of the District of the Border and based in Kansas City, saying he believed Shelby was at Pineville with 1,800 men. While the troop estimate had become more accurate (apparently Schofield no longer believed Shelby was rendezvousing with Cabell), Pineville is more than 50 miles southwest of Shelby's actual position on that date. Schofield thought Shelby would turn west towards Kansas, perhaps hitting the Federal base at Fort Scott. In fact, Shelby was heading straight for the heart of Missouri.

On October 5, the raiders came to Greenfield, where the town's 50 militiamen had barricaded themselves in the courthouse. As at Neosho, the defenders quickly surrendered when they saw they faced artillery, and Shelby's men fired the building. Col Coffee objected to this act because Greenfield was his hometown and he had practiced law there. He ordered his men to remove the law records and place them in the safekeeping of the county judge. The raiders then fell on the small fort at Stockton, compelling the militia to surrender and destroying the fort. The next day they scattered the militia at Humansville and Lt Thomas Keithley led ten scouts to Osceola, where they surprised a Federal garrison five times their number. The bluecoats didn't even try to hold their fortified position and fled the town. Keithley and his men burned the fort and returned to the main body. In two days Shelby's men had driven off four different Union detachments, destroyed three fortified locations, and captured an unknown number of mounts, weapons, and pieces of equipment, as well as 30 wagons of commissary supplies. This last acquisition was important. Shelby's men lived off the land, bringing very little food with them. On their grueling rides they usually didn't have time to forage like foot soldiers, or even sit down to a proper meal at a friendly secessionist home, like many guerrillas. One of their main sources of food was the supplies they captured from the enemy.

The easy victories were not to last. On the same day as Shelby's numerous little conquests, Schofield received his first accurate report. Col John Edwards wired his commander in St. Louis to report the attack on Greenfield and that the raiders were headed northeast. Schofield ordered BrigGen Thomas Davies, commanding at Rolla, to gather his cavalry at Lebanon in preparation for Shelby's eventual return to Arkansas. Meanwhile, Col Edwards gathered together 1,250 Union troops and three cannon and pursued the raiders. He reached Greenfield on the 7th, and continued on Shelby's trail all the way to Quincy before Schofield told them to break off pursuit and instead wait until Shelby moved back south. The trap was already being laid.

OCTOBER 4
1863

Shelby
attacks Neosho,
Missouri

The Baxter Springs Massacre

As these events were unfolding, rebel bushwhacker William Quantrill was in Kansas distracting the Union forces there in order to draw off men from pursuing Shelby. Quantrill was one of the Civil War's more curious characters. As a young man this Ohio schoolteacher cut off all ties with his friends and relations and headed to Bleeding Kansas. He fought on both sides during that conflict, apparently more for money than principle. When the war started he took the side of the South. His band grew in size and viciousness and included such leading guerrillas as "Bloody Bill" Anderson and Frank James. His hit-and-run raids were a major headache for Union commanders in the region and culminated in the August 21, 1863, raid on Lawrence, a leading abolitionist town in Kansas. There his men plundered the shops, burned a large number of the buildings, and killed 200 mostly unarmed men and boys.

This action was the worst atrocity against civilians in the Civil War and shocked people on both sides. In response, Gen Ewing issued General Order Number 11, forcing most civilians to leave the Missouri border counties south of the Missouri River. The idea was to stop local support for the guerrillas, but it led to a great deal of misery for the civilian population. Shelby's use of Quantrill was controversial then and continues to be so among historians today. Despite what the bushwhacker claimed, Quantrill had no official standing in the Confederate army and was fighting the war "on his own hook." Shelby's association with Quantrill strengthened the case of those in the North who wanted to brand Shelby as a guerrilla. Shelby may have held his nose at some of Quantrill's escapades, but he was a practical man and knew Quantrill could win battles.

Quantrill had been lurking in the western Missouri counties that had been cleared out by General Order Number 11. The order had done its job. While Quantrill's men were able to scavenge food from abandoned farms

OCTOBER 5 1863

Attacks on Greenfield and Stockton

Martial Law, painted by Missourian George Caleb Bingham in 1870, depicts Ewing's General Order Number 11. The order virtually depopulated several Missouri counties bordering Kansas and was in reprisal for Quantrill's Lawrence Massacre. The idea was to stop bushwhacking by removing the guerrillas' civilian support network. All it did was to shift guerrilla operations to other counties. (LoC)

The famous outlaw Frank James rode with Quantrill's bushwhackers and was at the Lawrence and Baxter Springs massacres. He's shown here in a photograph taken in 1898, long after his career as a bandit had ended. His younger brother Jesse was also a Confederate guerrilla. After Jesse was assassinated, Frank was able to reconcile himself with the law thanks to the efforts of John Newman Edwards. He never spent a day in jail for his crimes and led a quiet life until his death in 1915. (LoC)

and strayed animals, however, he lacked any civilian spies to warn him of Union movements. He found himself in numerous scrapes not of his choosing and ended up looking for greener pastures in Kansas.

Quantrill rendezvoused with his scattered detachments on September 30, gathering about 300 men. Among their number were many new recruits – Confederate army deserters and veterans, displaced secessionist civilians, and various wanderers. Col John Holt arrived with about 200 men, many of them new recruits, on orders to assist Shelby by distracting the Union command in Kansas and reduce the likelihood of Missouri getting reinforcements from that state. Holt was an experienced recruiter, but acted more like a bushwhacker than regular soldier; he had accompanied Quantrill on the raid on Lawrence. Unlike Quantrill, however, he really did hold a commission from the Confederate army. Technically he ranked Quantrill, but of course the rough-and-ready bushwhackers looked to Quantrill for direction.

On October 2 they crossed the state line, and four days later descended upon a pair of Federal soldiers driving a lumber wagon, from whom they learned of the existence of a new Union fort at Baxter Springs. The guerrillas dispatched their prisoners – bushwhackers and Federals had long since stopped showing each other mercy – and went to investigate.

Fort Blair stood on the north slope of a small valley. Four-foot-tall earthen embankments strengthened by logs ran a hundred feet on three of the sides. The western wall, by contrast, had been cleared away in order to expand the fort, but this hadn't been done yet and the fort was nothing more than a giant "c" shape. Most of the command and all the horses were away on a scouting mission, a mission that failed to notice Quantrill's approach. Remaining at the "fort" were 45 white soldiers and 50 members of the 2nd Kansas Colored Volunteers. All were scattered about, some in the camp inside the ramparts, some gathering around the cooking tent at a nearby stream, others wandering around. Their arms were stacked in camp. Their commander, Lt James Pond, sat eating in his tent some 200yds west of the fort.

Quantrill sent a detachment under Dave Poole and William Gregg to approach the fort from the east (being unaware of the opening in the west) and went with the rest of his men into the woods to come at the fort from the north. While Quantrill quickly became lost, Poole and Gregg's men galloped towards the fort, pistols blazing. Pond and his troops hurried for the fort, but the guerrillas arrived so fast that many had to weave and duck through the charging horses to make it. Some of the 2nd Kansas Colored

Volunteers swung at the riders with their fists, an act of amazing bravery or utter desperation, or both. Once they made it back to the fort they discovered guerrillas riding around amid the tents, trading shots with the soldiers who had stayed in camp.

Pond made it to a 12-pdr mountain howitzer that had recently been supplied to the fort. Neither he nor anyone else knew how to use it, but he turned out to be a fast learner and lobbed three shells into the guerrillas' line just as they formed for another charge. Meanwhile, those guerrillas already in the fort were being fired at from all sides and galloped out. Faced with a cannon and determined resistance, the guerrillas kept their distance. Pond would earn the Congressional Medal of Honor for his role in this fight, although he had to wait until 1898 for it to be awarded.

Meanwhile, Quantrill was having much better luck. Having become lost, he ended up several hundred yards north of the fort. There he spied a column of soldiers and wagons in the distance. It was none other than MajGen James Blunt, Union commander of the District of the Frontier, on his way to Fort Scott with part of his staff, a hundred mounted soldiers, his headquarters records, a brass band, a reporter, and a woman off to visit a sick husband in the army. Blunt and his entourage were completely unaware of the battle because the fort lay in a hollow and that location, combined with the intervening woods, muffled the sound of gunfire. He ordered the brass band in their special wagon to the front so he could treat the residents of Fort Blair to a few tunes.

Then Blunt spotted a group of blue-clad riders emerging from the woods to the east. It was Quantrill and his men, still lost. Blunt counted about a hundred riders and assumed they were a welcoming party from the fort. As they formed a ragged line and walked their horses towards him, Blunt began to wonder. Something didn't seem quite right. Perhaps it was the poor formation they held, or the officers riding up and down the line barking orders, or the large numbers of Colt Navy revolvers the newcomers carried – that was the favored weapon of bushwhackers, and wearing Federal blue was a favorite trick for getting in close.

Blunt formed up his own men and, still unsure, he himself rode forward to reconnoiter. He made it 50yds when the Kansas breeze brought him the sound of distant gunshots. A second line, twice as big as the first, emerged from the woods. Now 300 riders walked steadily towards him. At a range of 200yds the riders raised their guns and let out a volley at the isolated Blunt and his tiny command. Blunt wheeled in his saddle to give the order to fire

Jesse James fought for the South as a bushwhacker. It's unclear if he joined Quantrill in the autumn of 1863, and thus was present at the Baxter Springs fight, or joined the band of "Bloody Bill" Anderson after Quantrill's group broke up that winter. He certainly rode with Anderson after the breakup. He's shown here in 1864 in the typical guerrilla "bushwhacker shirt," a loose outer garment with large pockets for ammunition and spare cylinders for his Colt Navy revolvers. (LoC)

back and saw "with shame and humiliation ... the whole line broken, and all of them in full gallop over the prairie, completely panic stricken."

Blunt galloped back to his men, shouting at them to halt, but it was no use. The men scattered in all directions as the guerrillas, mounted on the best horses they could steal, closed in on them. Experts at firing from horseback, the guerrillas picked off the bluecoats as they tried to escape, emptying saddle after saddle and leaving a trail of dead and dying men scattered across the prairie. "They killed our men as fast as they caught them, sparing none," one survivor remembered.

But there weren't too many to remember. Bushwhackers were given no quarter by a direct order from the Union command in Missouri, and so they gave none in return. The wagon full of elegantly clad musicians, their ceremonial swords and brocade gleaming in the Kansas sun, was pursued by a lone bushwhacker. One musician pulled out a pistol and blasted him off his horse. This enraged the other bushwhackers and soon a whole crowd was chasing the wagon. Just as they were gaining ground, one of the wagon's wheels flew off and the musicians tumbled to the ground. The bushwhackers showed them no mercy. Every single one was gunned down, including a 12-year-old drummer boy, who didn't die from his gunshot wound but from the flames generated when the bushwhackers set the wagon on fire, with him underneath it.

Blunt whipped his horse and pounded away from the swarming killers. He took a wide gully at a full gallop and while his horse made it, the jolt of

Quantrill's raid on Lawrence, which killed 200 mostly unarmed men and boys and left the town in flames, started a new chapter in the Trans-Mississippi theater. The Union command responded by evicting the majority of civilians from the Missouri border counties to keep them from supporting guerrillas, and this led to even more violent reprisals from the bushwhackers. While considered a sideshow of the war, Missouri suffered more than most states. (LoC)

the landing threw Blunt from the saddle and he continued for a full mile hanging onto the horse's neck, not daring to stop. The woman in the column, a Mrs Thomas, hid in the back of her buggy and her driver urged the horses across the rolling prairie. They made it away unscathed, the buggy riddled with bullet holes.

Back at the scene of the carnage, Quantrill and his men found many of their victims had been carrying whiskey and they threw themselves a big party. Quantrill was exultant. He mistook the fine but blood-spattered uniform of a lieutenant-colonel for that of Blunt and crowed drunkenly, "By god, Shelby could not whip Blunt. Neither could Marmaduke. But I whipped him!" Other

**OCTOBER 6
1863**

Attacks on Humansville and Osceola

A period sketch of a "jerilla." The picture is also labeled "a deserter". There was often little difference and some deserters attacked anyone who looked worth robbing. Shelby loathed these bandits but worked with guerrillas like William Quantrill, who despite being one of the most brutal bushwhackers was at least consistent in attacking Unionists. (LoC)

guerrillas acted in a similar fashion. One danced a jig on a wounded soldier who managed to play possum and eventually escaped to tell the tale. Others peppered wounded men with bullets. One guerrilla, 15-year-old Riley Crawford, thought he'd make a joke by going up to what he assumed was a corpse, smacked the body with a cavalry saber, and shouted "Get up, you Federal son of a bitch!" Riley gaped as the man actually did get up. He'd been playing dead like some of the others and thought he'd been spotted. Riley whipped out a revolver and shot him down.

Eventually Quantrill got his men together and plundered the wagon and corpses for food, uniforms, weapons, and all of Blunt's papers. He decided not to attack the fort again and moved out towards Texas. The leaves were beginning to turn and soon would fall. Then the thick brush of Missouri and eastern Kansas would provide no cover. Texas had become the winter playground for the bushwhackers, and Quantrill decided he and his men had done enough for the Confederate cause that year.

Union losses were seven dead and 23 wounded at the fort, plus a Pony Express rider who happened to be there was killed. Two other civilians, a woman and child, were wounded. Of Blunt's group 82 lay dead and 13 were wounded. Five of the latter, suffering from multiple wounds, later died.

Mounting Resistance

On October 7, Shelby's column approached Warsaw, a town situated on a bluff on the north bank of the Osage River. The Federal garrison, although outnumbered, was in position on the north side covering the ford. Shelby sent Gordon's 200 men on a wide loop across another ford and around the town to come at the Federals from behind. He then deployed Hunter's, Hooper's, and Shanks' men straight across the ford. For half an hour the bluecoats put up a dogged defense and the frontal assault made no headway until Gordon arrived from the north and put the Federals to flight. Shelby now crossed the Osage, having made it more than 300 miles in 15 days. At Warsaw he captured 30 wagonloads of arms and food and ten prisoners. The raiders helped themselves to anything they liked from the shops and confiscated $400 from the bank. Yet the determined defense of the ford was an ominous sign. Resistance was stiffening.

It was also getting more organized. While Ewing and Blunt were entangled with Quantrill's guerrillas in Kansas and Schofield was still concentrating men at Fort Scott and far western Missouri, some Union commanders were waking up to the real threat. BrigGen Egbert Brown, who had fought Shelby and Marmaduke at Springfield earlier in the year, moved with 800 men of the 7th Missouri State Militia Cavalry and a section of artillery to Osceola, hoping to head off Shelby before he crossed the Osage. Hearing that Shelby was already at Warsaw, he sent 200 men under Maj Emory Foster in pursuit, with orders to keep him informed of Shelby's route. Brown then hurried with the rest of his force to Sedalia, making the 65-mile trip to the northeast by dawn on the 9th. Brown realized that to catch Shelby he'd have to ride as hard as the raiders. Foster, fearing that Brown might not make it to Sedalia in time, took a back road, bypassed Shelby's column, and

got between the raiders and Sedalia. His cavalry dragged branches behind their horses and kicked up so much dust that Shelby thought Brown's entire force was close by. Not wanting to engage in a set-piece battle, Shelby headed to the railroad stop at Tipton instead. Foster was also able to wound two of Shelby's scouts and capture three. Foster didn't execute the prisoners, but felt obliged to explain to his superior officer that he didn't kill them because Shelby had captured some of his men. The fact that an officer had to make excuses for not killing prisoners shows how brutal the war in Missouri had become.

Another quick thinker was LtCol Bazel Lazear, who at the head of about 500 men of the 1st Missouri State Militia Cavalry, left Warrensburg on October 7 and moved to Clinton in the hope of running into the rebels. Getting there the next day, he received intelligence that Shelby had taken Warsaw and was headed north. Brown had ordered Lazear south to Osceola, but instead he headed to Calhoun 11 miles to the northeast. Lazear correctly anticipated Shelby's next move and was on a path to intersect with him. If he had obeyed orders, he'd have been going in the opposite direction. At Calhoun, Lazear received the bonus of an extra 70 cavalrymen who had been pushed out of Warsaw.

More men were on the march. BrigGen Odon Guitar led the 9th Missouri State Militia Cavalry regiment to Boonville, an important river port in the Little Dixie region. Kansas gathered troops to send to central Missouri, as did St. Louis. Jefferson City was reinforced by the 1st Nebraska Cavalry, the 7th Enrolled Missouri Militia, and a thousand cavalrymen from Colorado. Schofield was receiving persistent requests for reinforcements from MajGen

Quantrill's raiders burnt much of Lawrence, Kansas. It wasn't the only town burnt in the region. Several others were torched by Union and Confederate troops, guerrillas, or bandits. Union troops and Kansas jayhawkers often did this to farms or even entire settlements that had shown support for rebels, and Confederates and guerrillas often did the same thing to loyalist homes and towns. Such acts were generally perpetrated by irregulars or mid-ranking officers, and rarely ended in any punishment for the perpetrators. Warsaw, Missouri, where Shelby fought a skirmish, had only one building standing at the end of the war, a tavern used as the local Union headquarters. (LoC)

William Rosecrans, mired in the Chattanooga campaign. Schofield had none to give. The state capital at Jefferson City and all of central Missouri was under threat from a completely unanticipated attack. One of Shelby's main goals of the raid had been achieved.

While the resistance gathered, the rebels enjoyed easy times on the 8th and 9th as they passed through a rich German settlement in and around Cole Camp. The Germans assumed these mostly blue-clad riders were Union soldiers, and as they were plied with beer and sausage Shelby's men saw no reason to enlighten the friendly farmers. The bluff ended when the rebels found large herds of fine horses and exchanged them for their own weary mounts. In the troubled wartime state of Missouri, hospitality was rarely rewarded.

On the night of October 9, Shelby sent Capt James Wood and 100 men to destroy the railroad bridge over the Lamine River. This bridge stood 15 miles east of Sedalia, an important regional center and at that time the terminus of the line. The bridge had been heavily fortified early in the war with a massive set of earthworks that can still be seen today. It had been thought that there would be a major battle there, but when none came the earthworks were abandoned and the bridge protected in the usual manner with a blockhouse. Only 28 men guarded it. Wood found most of the defenders asleep and came upon them so quickly that the soldiers surrendered without firing a shot. Wood's men burned both the blockhouse and the bridge. John Newman Edwards reported that, "In five minutes not an armed enemy was near, and in five minutes more this magnificent structure, reared at the cost of $400,000, stood tenable against the midnight sky, one mass of hissing, seething, liquid fire." Here was Edwards in rare form. He loved nothing better than a Union defeat, even if the bridge really only cost $9,000.

On the morning of the 10th, Shelby's scouts tried to stop a train on the Missouri Pacific Railroad 2 miles west of Tipton. On board was LtCol Thomas Crittenden, commander of the 7th Missouri State Militia Cavalry, who was checking to see if the railroad was secure. He got his answer in the form of a volley. The train quickly reversed back to Tipton and Crittenden ordered an evacuation of the small garrison there. In happier times, Crittenden had been a guest at Shelby's wedding, and in the future he would be the Missouri governor who would make a deal with Robert Ford to assassinate Jesse James. Shelby soon showed up at Tipton, capturing stragglers and abandoned supplies. His raiders quickly burned the railroad depot and wrecked the water tower. As they loaded goods from the local shops onto their supply wagons, some civilians noted that the wagons, which they said were six in number, were driven by blacks. There's no mention in the Confederate records of these drivers and they may have been runaway slaves or free blacks conscripted along the way.

Edwards reports Shelby sent out "a cloud of scouts, ordering them to do their worst upon both telegraph and railroad. For 30 miles either way, rails were torn up, ties burned, bridges destroyed, wire carried off, and cattle-stops and water tanks obliterated." They would remain to plague the local Unionists until Shelby headed south again.

OCTOBER 7 1863

Attack on Warsaw

Back in Tipton, Shelby had his own work to do. Two hundred men of the 5th Provisional EMM and an equal number from the 4th Missouri State Militia Cavalry drove in his pickets. These inexperienced militiamen, however, proved no match for Shelby's spirited counterattack and soon fled, harassed for several miles by Shelby's raiders. They joined up with Lazear later that night, bringing his force up to almost a thousand men. Shelby now had a serious threat close behind him.

Shelby swung 5 miles west to gobble up another small garrison at Syracuse before heading north towards the Missouri River. Jefferson City was only 40 miles to the east, but Shelby's scouts reported the state capital was guarded by 8,000 men behind strong earthworks and forts. Instead he headed for Boonville, just 20 miles due north. This prosperous Missouri River port was a strong center of secessionist sentiment in the Little Dixie region. Shelby had been picking up some recruits along the way, but his fast pace through the countryside hampered his ability to gather very many. He hoped that at a larger town he could rally a more to the Southern cause.

Negotiating a "slippery, miry road" soaked by the previous night's rain, and halting for three hours to fix a broken axle on the Parrott rifle, Shelby arrived at Boonville midday on the 11th. During the march, his rearguard had skirmished with Lazear's advance scouts of the 1st Missouri State Militia

OCTOBER 9 1863

Raiders burn Lamine railroad bridge

The 9th Missouri State Militia Cavalry, commanded by BrigGen Odon Guitar. Few photos exist of Missouri state militia units, and this rare view shows the men's uniforms mixed with items of civilian clothing. (Courtesy State Historical Society of Missouri)

An unidentified African-American soldier in front of a painted backdrop showing weapons and an American flag at Benton Barracks, St. Louis. Several thousand blacks volunteered for service in the Trans-Mississippi, and many more worked as laborers for the Union army. If captured, they were generally killed or returned to slavery. (LoC)

Cavalry, now hot on the raiders' trail. Once they saw Shelby make it into Boonville, they reported back to Lazear.

The weary raiders were greeted as heroes by the mostly Southern townspeople. Some men took a break to be treated to meals in private homes, while others looted two Unionist merchants of $4,000 each in supplies. They also found an iron 4-pdr artillery piece, but there being no ammunition, they destroyed it.

Shelby's raiders took a short break from their holiday to repulse 250 men of the 9th Missouri State Militia Cavalry led by Maj Reeves Leonard. They were part of Odon Guitar's outfit – the "Bloody Ninth" – a nickname they earned defeating guerrillas and rebel recruiting parties. They tried to cross from the north bank of the river in a small steam-powered ferry that could only hold 50 men and their horses, but a Unionist civilian shouted out to them that Shelby was in town and the boat immediately turned around. The raiders hurried down to the shore and started sniping at it. As the vessel chugged out of range, Shelby's 6-pdr was unlimbered and opened fire, hitting the boat twice. The pilot ducked for cover and Maj Leonard had to take the wheel and steer the boat to the north shore. The soldiers soon disembarked and hurried out of range of the cannon. The raiders would hear more from them soon.

Later the steamboat *Isabella* appeared, bearing LtCol Crittenden and a detachment of the 7th Missouri State Militia Cavalry. Shelby's men tried to lure them ashore, but Crittenden wasn't fooled and turned the boat back around and landed a short distance downriver.

In the meantime, more Union troops were moving in from the east as BrigGen Brown realized he may have Shelby trapped. With the north blocked by the wide and unfordable Missouri River, and troops closing in, the Union commander must have felt he'd run him to ground at last. BrigGen Ewing was supposed to be marching in from the west, but neither Brown nor Shelby knew how far he had advanced. Communication between the scattered Union troops had become difficult. Shelby had cut down many of the telegraph lines, and the guerrillas had cut down even more in support of his raid. Union detachments had to rely on couriers. These lone riders often got bushwhacked, their bodies left in lonely ravines, their messages never delivered.

Shelby heard of these maneuvers and decided in the late afternoon to leave Boonville. Just when speed was of the essence, Shelby's Parrott gun broke again, requiring time-consuming repairs. While his artillerists struggled to fix it, LtCol Lazear's entire force appeared and drove in Shelby's pickets.

Shelby sent Col Hooper and his 200 men to stop the bluecoats. They managed to keep Lazear out of town until long after nightfall. The repairs finally complete, Shelby pulled his men out of Boonville to a point 4 miles west along the road to Marshall and made camp. The firing between Hooper and Lazear had died down by this point, and Hooper disengaged and joined his commander.

Exhausted by their long journey, the raiders slept heavily. All except Shelby. Edwards, who usually put his hero on the highest of pedestals, must have been speaking the truth when he said that Shelby barely slept at all due to the "incessant agony of his wounded and suppurating arm, carried constantly in a sling during all the extraordinary fatigue and cold of the rapid march." Lazear's men slept where they were, without food or fire or tents, and in the line of battle where they had last fired on Hooper's men. They resumed the chase in the morning, getting an early reward with the discovery of two of Shelby's men eating breakfast at a house just west of Boonville. As the surprised raiders appeared at the front door, the soldiers shot them dead.

Other units were closing in. Brown was 10 miles southwest of Boonville with 1,600 men and four or six pieces of artillery. Local units rallied to join Brown and Lazear. The latter received 120 men of the 9th Provisional EMM under Capt W.D. Wear on the night of October 11. Large forces mobilized from St. Louis and Kansas City. Looking at their maps, the Union and Confederate commanders saw that Shelby had gotten himself into a cul-de-sac. The Missouri River lay to the north, impassable. To the west the Lamine River flowed from the south into the Missouri. There was a ford over this part of the Lamine, but Shelby was unsure if Ewing had made it there yet. He knew Brown's forces were to the southwest and Lazear's to the east.

Army blacksmiths near Tipton, Missouri. While Union cavalry was well equipped with blacksmithing equipment and horseshoes, this was yet another area where the Confederate army's supplies ran short. Shelby often had to leave a portion of his command back at base for lack of horseshoes. (LoC)

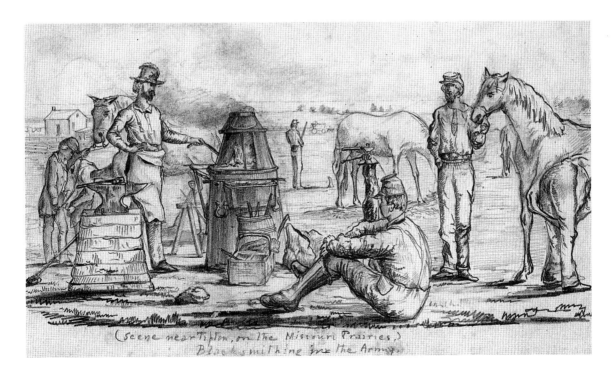

(scene near Tipton, on the Missouri Prairies)
Blacksmithing for the Army.

This 10-pdr Parrott rifle at Gettysburg is the same type used by Shelby on his raid. Its length of bore is 70in, diameter of bore is 2.9in, and total weight is 900lb. It had a crew of six. These rifled pieces were first produced in the North in 1860 and were copied by the South during the war. They were highly prized for their accuracy and range. The manual *Instruction For Field Artillery* from 1864 gives its maximum range as 6,200yds, while *Ranges Of Parrott Guns, And Notes For Practice*, 1863, gives a maximum range of 5,000yds. (Courtesy JackMelton.com)

OCTOBER 10 1863

Attack on Tipton

OCTOBER 12 1863

Morning attack by Lazear; ambush at Dug Ford; fight at Merrill's Crossing

The next morning (October 12), Maj Leonard and LtCol Crittenden finally crossed the river and landed at Boonville. They stayed in town long enough to have a meal before heading out. As the history of Cooper County states: "Boonville, then, was once more clear of troops, and the citizens had time to gather together provisions to feed the next lot of hungry soldiers who happened to land there, whether they were federals or confederates."

As the sun rose on the 12th, Lazear woke up the rebel camp with a fierce attack on Shelby's pickets. The entire camp was aroused within moments and Shelby ordered his men to form up for battle. Lazear, however, didn't confront them. He was playing for time, hoping Brown would get in front of the rebels and trap them. Shelby realized no battle was coming at that moment and headed down the road towards Marshall. Lazear followed, skirmishing with the Confederate rearguard the entire way. The raiders lost eight killed and four taken prisoner, while Lazear lost only two dead and two wounded.

Brown hadn't moved in front of Shelby; in fact he moved 8 miles south of Boonville thinking that the raiders would head east out of the trap. He planned to link up with Lazear and make a stand there. Brown had been working on a false rumor, probably spread by Shelby himself. Shelby couldn't have headed east in any case, as Lazear was too close on his tail. Here was another case of Union officers not communicating effectively with one another and not clearly anticipating Shelby's next move. Although Brown moved in the wrong direction, he did send a small number of cavalry to the southwest, and they ended up skirmishing with Shelby's forward scouts. Once Brown's main force got into position, he realized Shelby was moving southwest rather than east and immediately ordered a countermarch. Much time had been lost and the trap would have to wait to be sprung. Meanwhile, Shelby was planning a trap of his own.

Odon Guitar marched with Alexander Doniphan's famous 1st Missouri Mounted Volunteers in the Mexican–American War. He was also a lawyer, a gold prospector in California, and a prominent Whig politician. Although a slave owner, he joined the North to preserve the Union. He formed a regiment of volunteers that became the 9th Missouri State Militia Cavalry and defeated numerous Confederate recruiters and guerrillas. For this he was brevetted a brigadier-general. He is seen here with an unidentified woman. (Courtesy State Historical Society of Missouri)

Ambush at Dug Ford

Shelby's scouts discovered Ewing hadn't made it to the Lamine and the entire column was able to cross at Dug Ford. Here he found an excellent spot from which to delay the pursuit. The ford of the narrow river had steep banks 10ft high on each side, made slick by the passage of his horses. On the west bank, thick foliage, trees, stumps, rough ground, and fallen logs limited visibility to almost zero.

Shelby detached Maj Gordon with his 200 men to hold the west bank and delay the Union pursuit. Gordon placed some of his men on the east bank and dismounted the rest and hid them on the west bank with their horses well out of sight. When the Union force arrived from the east, the mounted men fired a single volley and retreated across the river in apparent disorder. The Union troops gave chase across the river. Once they were almost to the other

OCTOBER 13 1863

Battle of Marshall

Railroad bridges proved especially vulnerable to attacks by guerrillas and cavalry raiders. This one is similar to the Lamine River bridge Shelby's men destroyed. (LoC)

side, their horses struggling with the water and the steep bank, the rest of Gordon's men rose up from their hiding places and delivered a powerful volley from close range. In his official report, Lazear compared it to a thunderclap. Edwards is typically effusive:

> All the bed of the creek was filled by horsemen twenty and thirty deep, while more were pouring up from behind eager to become engaged. Into this solid, compact mass of human flesh tore the bullets from two hundred rifles not ten rods distant, while revolvers were used with incessant and deadly effect. It was a ghastly and horrible sight. Dying men, wounded horses, mutilated riders were struggling, screaming, writhing and drowning in the water and mud of the river, while those yet untouched rode down their unfortunate comrades in furious efforts to escape.

Edwards claims that 111 Union soldiers died in this engagement and only one Confederate was wounded. The official Union report, which is almost certainly much closer to the truth, states only two soldiers died and five were wounded, one mortally, while the rebels had "five or six" wounded, some mortally. The anonymous author of the history of Saline County, who said he interviewed participants on both sides and the Federal surgeon who cared for the wounded, put the Federal loss at "eight to ten men killed, and three times that many wounded." Whatever their losses, the Union pursuit was smashed and would take some time before it got organized again, giving Shelby's men some much-needed breathing room. But not much. Lazear was still alive and determined to run Shelby down.

Into the Trap

So was Brown. He was moving in the same direction as Lazear but 2 miles to the south, struggling through terrain that Brown described as "very broken and hilly, with narrow gorges and dense brush." Brown feared getting stopped by a detachment of well-placed raiders, and he hurried forward. He crossed the Lamine south of Dug Ford without encountering opposition and turned north. After linking up with Lazear, he took the vanguard as his men were fresher. He hit Shelby's rearguard and fought a running skirmish with it for several miles.

Suffering constant harassment to his rear, Shelby decided to make a stand at Merrill's Crossing on Salt Fork Creek near Jonesborough, about 9 miles southeast of Marshall. This clash would not be another skirmish but a full-on fight. Shelby ordered his 6-pdr smoothbore and 10-pdr Parrott rifle unlimbered. Brown unlimbered four 4-pdr smoothbores and deployed his men. The ensuing artillery duel killed one Confederate and a Union gunner, the latter who died after a cannonball took off both his legs.

Shelby slowly gave ground, being pushed until he was only 6 miles east of Marshall. Both sides must have been seriously fatigued by this point, and a freezing downpour added to their misery. The fight and the rain continued until darkness. As usual, Edwards' and the Union's reports differ widely. Edwards talks in glowing terms of silencing Brown's guns and driving him several miles, a trail of blue-coated bodies behind him. This is obviously untrue as it was Shelby, not Brown, who gave ground, although Shelby was trying to keep on the move and the progress towards Marshall may only have been a tactical retreat with the intention to escape. Brown claimed to have killed 16 Confederates and lost only one man killed. It's difficult to see how Brown could have known the exact number of Confederate casualties, since his troops were engaged in a running battle over rough terrain during a rainstorm. Distorted figures are common in Civil War reports, especially in the Trans-Mississippi theater. Commanders exaggerated enemy numbers and losses, and downplayed their own casualties.

With a dreary day turning into a cold and wet night, Shelby rested his men. Brown's troops lay down in the line of battle and slept on their weapons to keep them dry from the rain. Still looking for an opening in the rapidly closing noose, Shelby sent 300 riders to Arrow Rock. They found no enemy forces present and took the opportunity to ransack the town. They returned with their report, but by then it was too late for Shelby to make a break for the east. The noose had tightened further, even more than Shelby realized.

When Brown had started skirmishing with Shelby's rearguard, Lazear had tried to rest his men and horses, who had been going almost nonstop for days. Just as they were cooking their first meal in 36 hours, they heard the boom of the artillery duel at Merrill's Crossing. They must have groaned and complained, but they wolfed down their half-cooked meal, mounted their weary steeds, and joined the fray. They arrived just as the sky darkened from gray to black. They lay down for their second night of sleeping on their arms but were awakened before 0500hrs and told to move out. Lazear had spent the past two hours in conference with Maj Foster, who had received orders from BrigGen Brown to send Lazear and his men on a quick ride southwest around Shelby's flank and take up positions at the town of Marshall. Brown would continue the pursuit and drive Shelby into Lazear's arms.

OVERLEAF: Surprise attack near Boonville. At dawn on October 12, 1863, Shelby's pursuers finally caught up with him. Union soldiers attacked his camp while he was still preparing for the day and drove in his pickets. Shelby hastily assembled his men into line of battle, but found that the Union attack was only a probe. Once Shelby realized a full attack was not imminent, he broke away and continued his march.

It was now October 13, the day the Union pursuit finally trapped Shelby's raiders. By 0700hrs Lazear was in position, forming his lines on a chain of steep hills fronted by ravines just to the east of Marshall. Edwards remembers the battlefield "rent and broken by huge gullies, and covered with a thick growth of hazel bushes, was peculiarly unfitted for the desperate charge Col. Shelby intended to make." Lazear sent out pickets on every road nearby and sent 200 men under Maj Kelly to the ford of the Salt Fork River a mile to the east of town, the most likely spot where Shelby would appear since the raiders had been following the course of the river since Jonesborough. As Kelly's men peered through the thick brush looking for the raiders, or foraged apples and cabbages from nearby farms, the rest of Lazear's men cooked another meal. The official records don't say if they managed to get it fully cooked or not. Even if they did, it would have been a quick meal, because Shelby was almost in town.

The Battle of Marshall

The combined Union force numbered about 2,800 men. Lazear had 1,020 men and two cannon in front of Shelby and Brown had 1,800 men and six guns coming up behind Shelby. Brown hoped to trap the raiders between the two forces.

Shelby crossed Salt Fork Creek and left Shanks with 200 men to protect the creek and tear up the bridge. Shelby then skirmished with Kelly's 200 men of the 4th Missouri State Militia Cavalry, sent to delay him while Lazear moved the rest of his force in line. Kelly formed a skirmish line across the road just west of the river leading to Marshall, and positioned the rest of his men in a ravine parallel to the road. As Shelby's vanguard came up the road, thinking they'd easily scatter the skirmish line, they were hit by fire from the ravine on their left. Four raiders were wounded, one mortally. This clash forced Shelby to stop, dismount, and form a line of battle, by which time Lazear had formed his own lines. Kelly then withdrew to act as Lazear's reserve.

Shelby proceeded to probe Lazear's lines, first with Hooper going against Maj J.H. McGhee's 200 men of the 1st Missouri State Militia Cavalry positioned on a hill southeast of town. Hooper's advance was hampered by a deep and brushy ravine, and he soon fell back under heavy fire. Next, Elliot's scouts and Gordon's men attacked the Union center held by Maj Mullins and his 300 men of the 1st Missouri State Militia Cavalry, who threw back three Confederate charges. Then Hunter and Coffee attacked Maj Gentry and his 200 men of the 5th Provisional Enrolled Missouri Militia, who formed the Union left. Gentry's inexperienced militia fled without firing a shot. The Union artillery between Mullins and Gentry had to pull back to avoid capture. Gentry managed to rally his men at the edge of town and held off several more charges. Kelly moved to Gentry's left to strengthen the Union line.

After the battle had been going on for an hour and a half, Brown's force appeared on the scene. Brown sent Maj T.W. Houts with 300 men and two 6-pdrs against Shanks, who was positioned on the west side of the bridge over Salt Fork Creek with Shelby's artillery. While they didn't have time to completely destroy the little bridge before Brown's men showed up, the rebels had a good position on high ground covered in undergrowth and commanding the ford. Houts set up his artillery and shelled Shanks' position. One shot smashed right through the trail of the Parrott and the raiders had to repair it quickly with a makeshift trail made of poles.

The fighting at the creek raged on, but Brown could make no headway. He left Houts in command at the creek and sent Capt Foster, Maj Seuss, and Maj Foster with 700 men and two pieces of artillery across the river ½ mile to the north to hit Shanks in the flank. Meanwhile, Col J.F. Philips crossed with his 800 men of the 7th Missouri State Militia Cavalry ¾ mile to the south. Philips moved slowly through the ravines and tangled brush and was forced to dismount. When they got almost within rifle range of Shelby's main Confederate force, Philips saw them preparing to withdraw. At this point Philips remounted his men, moved through the clearer land south of town, passed through town, and ended up to the left of Kelly to stop the anticipated rebel breakout.

It was now about 1000hrs. Shanks saw he was outnumbered and flanked and made a fighting retreat towards the main rebel body with Houts harassing him the entire way. He never reached his commander, though, because Shelby mounted his force and prepared to break through the Union left and flee northwest. This maneuver took an hour because of the thick underbrush, numerous ravines and the need to build a makeshift bridge over one especially deep ravine so his wagons could cross. The trail of the Parrott broke again, and a frustrated Shelby ordered it spiked. By the time Shelby finally got going, Philips had established his new position to the left of Kelly.

As Shelby moved out, his black plume bobbing in the gun smoke and riding a fresh horse after one had been shot from underneath him, Kelly remounted his men and charged. Kelly neatly cut the rebel force in half. Shelby, Gordon, Coffee, and Elliot's scouts retreated to the northwest while Shanks, Hunter, and Hooper headed northeast. While Kelly's charge looks impressive on paper, in reality the two bodies of rebels had already been separated with only about 20 of Gordon's rebels standing in Kelly's path. Kelly had little trouble scattering them and Philips soon followed him into the gap. Shelby and his column were already headed northwest. They had to pass through Gentry's militia, spread out to one man every 6ft in order to cover both their section of the line and the space formerly occupied by Kelly. Shelby's raiders dispersed them with apparently no loss to either side. The rest of the rebels, led by Hunter, were still cut off. They had the 6-pdr and most of the wagons. Under pressure from all sides, they broke out in the opposite direction to Shelby.

Philips pursued Shelby's section for the rest of the day while Lazear moved his men west to intercept Shelby in case he turned south. Philips took two 6-pdrs with him but refused the offer of the four 4-pdrs, saying he'd "rather have four big clubs" than the undersized cannons. Houts chased after the sections of Hunter, Shanks, and Hooper. Both columns skirmished for the rest of the day with only light losses.

The Federals reported that the Iron Brigade lost 53 killed and 98 wounded and the Union had a total loss of only 42. Such small losses for a

OVERLEAF:
Trap at Dug Ford. On October 12, 1863, Shelby temporarily stopped his Union pursuers with a classic ambush. As Shelby crossed the Lamine River at Dug Ford, he saw the narrow river had steep banks 10ft high on each side, made slick by the passage of his men's horses. Thick foliage, trees, stumps, rough ground, and fallen logs limited visibility to almost zero on the west bank. Shelby detached Maj G.P. Gordon with about 200 men to hold the west bank and delay the Union pursuit. Gordon placed some of his men on the east bank. The rest he dismounted and hid on the west bank with their horses well out of sight to the rear. When the Union force arrived from the east, the mounted rebels fired a volley and retreated across the Lamine in apparent disorder. The Union troops dutifully galloped across the river, and once they were almost across, the rest of Gordon's men rose up and delivered a powerful fusillade from only a few yards away.

hard-fought battle lasting five hours were thanks to the thick brush covering much of the battlefield, and the stone wall behind which Lazear's men lay prone. The author of the Saline County history says "lead enough was thrown to kill and maim a division" but owing to the terrain, "firing was a mere pastime." He asserts, without citing sources, that only one Federal and four or five Confederates died.

The Saline County chronicler also reported a humorous incident concerning one of the civilians at Marshall:

> A Mr. McCafferty had some very choice pieces of bacon, which he was very anxious should not be captured or plundered by either side. His house was placed on blocks, without any underpinning. He thought to "save his bacon" by hiding it under the house. His neighbor, Jim McKown, had a pack of hounds, lean, lank and ravenously hungry. Affrighted at the noise of the battle, "the thunder of the captains and the shouting," these hounds had slunk under McCafferty's house, and lay cowering right where he proposed to hide his meat. As he flung it under piece by piece, the dogs seized it and gleefully carried it away to a place of safety, where it was devoured. McCafferty, strange to say (!) was laughed at by those of his neighbors who had no meat of their own to hide, as well as those who had, on account of his mishap.

Breaking Free

Shelby had gotten away, but his command had been divided, the Yankees were in hot pursuit, and they had more than 400 miles to ride to get back home. Philips boasted that the raiders were "running like wild hogs." Shelby was unsure if Hunter had escaped or had been captured. He waited an anxious hour, hoping the colonel would appear. When he didn't, Shelby made the agonizing decision to leave him. There wasn't really any choice in the matter.

After Hunter broke free he left a detachment under Capts Franklin and Langhorne to delay the pursuit as he and Shanks sat down with a map and tried to figure out the best escape route. After an hour they came up with a plan and headed out. The rearguard remained constantly engaged with the Federal cavalry and the stray column only made it 3 miles from the battlefield before the sun set.

Nightfall gave a brief respite. Men and horses ate their meager provisions, the last ammunition was doled out, and the brass 6-pdr, now the raiders' only artillery piece, was given a fresh team to pull it. Then they set out in the dark towards Florence. Remarkably, they met no trouble that night or most of the next day. It appears the Union command was too tired and confused to mount a successful pursuit, although the bluecoats continued to chase Shelby's main force.

Late on October 14, Hunter's group came upon a group of Federals guarding several forage wagons and 200 mules along the Pacific Railroad near Sedalia. The raiders chased off the Federals, had a quick snack from the wagons, and tore up the railroad. They burned the wagons and took many of the mules. As they entered Florence, however, they were ambushed by Union troops. After a brief moment of confusion, Hunter and Shanks' men rallied and beat off the attackers, then hurried on across the Osage River before another force could get into position and stop their crossing.

Not far south of the river they had another skirmish on October 15 at Cross Timbers and the next day at Deer Creek. Neither fight was a major one, merely a brief effort to scatter small, local forces. The Union's strategy of spreading small contingents across the countryside to quell the guerrilla threat was working in the raiders' favor. Later, on October 16, Hunter clashed with a force left behind by BrigGen John McNeil, commander of the Southwestern District of Missouri, at Humansville. What he didn't realize was that another Union force was in the area, and his rearguard was surprised. Several raiders were captured and Hunter had to spike his cannon in order to make a speedy escape – the team of horses had fallen dead from exhaustion and the raiders didn't have time to hitch up another team. The Iron Brigade had now lost both of its artillery pieces.

The next day Hunter and his men moved another 20 miles to a spot just north of Mount Vernon, where they found rich pickings at the farm of a captain of the Home Guard. Yankee grain and turkeys filled their bellies, but their rest was interrupted by a night attack. The men saddled up and dashed off into the dark, skirting Mount Vernon and its garrison and crossing the Wire Road. The next day they scattered a group of 200 Federals and made it to Berryville before resting.

While all this was going on, Shelby led his main column westwards under constant harassment from the 7th Missouri State Militia Cavalry under Philips. Shelby dealt with this threat by forming a two-squadron retreating defense. One group dismounted and held a defensive position while the other rode forward to find another good position. After a time the first squadron mounted up and retreated past the second squadron, which was now dismounted and holding a new position further down the road. Then the process repeated itself.

The fighting pursuit continued well into the evening until Shelby's local knowledge finally shook Philips off. As the Union militia advanced on Shelby, the raiders took a sudden turn to the right, exposing their flank. Philips urged his men forward into a charge, thinking he finally had Shelby where he wanted him, but instead, "before I knew it I had dashed into a vast swamp. Our horses sunk to the saddle girths, and before I could rescue myself and command and get remounted Shelby disappeared in the woods. No fox was more cunning and no wolf more tireless than he. Press on as we might we could not regain sight of him before night."

Philips slackened his pursuit. His men and horses were worn out and needed a rest. Shelby was resting too. He had made it to Hawkin's Mill and ordered a three-hour break. It was now dark, Philips was somewhere far behind, and there was no sign of any other Federal or militia units. Shelby knew that once the sun rose the chase would be on again in earnest, so he wanted to give his men a brief respite. He distributed 30 rounds per man from the wagons and then pushed the wagons into the Missouri River, along with two ambulances. He also left behind a herd of 40 mules. Then came the

CONFEDERATE FORCES **1**-**7**

1,350 men, all mounted. One 10-pound steel Parrott gun and one 6-pounder brass piece.

1 Col J.O. Shelby

2 Lt Col. J.C. Hooper: 200 men

3 Capt G.P. Gordon: 200 men

4 Maj Benjamin Elliot: 100 men.

5 Col D.C. Hunter: 200 men

6 Col J.T. Coffee: 400 men

7 Maj David Shanks: 200 men

Capt "Tuck" Thorpe: 50 scouts. There is no record of what they did during the battle

A wagon train of about two dozen wagons and two ambulances

STAGE ONE

On October 13, 1863, the Union forces of Missouri finally cornered Shelby's raiders and forced him to fight a pitched battle. Union militia under the command of LtCol Bazel Lazear had been closely pursuing Shelby for a couple of days, and on 11 October he was joined by BrigGen Egbert Brown's force. The combined Union force numbered about 2,800 men. On the night of 12 October, he sent Lazear and his 1,020 men ahead to cut off the raiders at the town of Marshall along the Salt Fork River while Brown kept up the pursuit. Brown hoped to trap Shelby between the two forces.

Lazear was able to reach Marshall by daybreak on the 13 October. Shelby soon arrived, crossing Salt Fork Creek and leaving Shanks to protect the river. Shelby then skirmished with Maj Kelly's 200 men of the Fourth Missouri State Militia Cavalry, sent to delay him while Lazear got the rest of his force in line. Kelly forced Shelby to stop, dismount, and form a line of battle, by which time Lazear had formed his own lines. Kelly then withdrew to act as a reserve behind Mullins. Shelby proceeded to probe Lazear's lines, first with Hooper going against McGhee's position on a hill southeast of town. Hooper's advance was hampered by a deep and brushy ravine and he soon fell back under heavy fire. Next, Elliot and Gordon attacked the Union center held by Mullins, who threw back three Confederate charges. Then Hunter and Coffee attacked Gentry's inexperienced militia, who fled without firing a shot. The Union artillery between Mullins and Gentry had to be pulled back to avoid capture. Gentry managed to rally his men at the edge of town and held off several more charges. Kelly moved to Gentry's left to strengthen the Union line.

By this time the battle had been going on an hour and a half and Brown's force appeared on the scene. Brown sent Houts with four pieces of artillery against Shanks, who was positioned on the west side of the bridge over Salt Fork Creek. Foster, Suess, and Foster with two pieces of artillery crossed the river ½ mile to the north to hit Shanks in the flank. Meanwhile Phillips crossed ¾ mile to the south. Phillips moved slowly through the ravines and tangled brush and was forced to dismount his men. When they got almost within rifle range of the main Confederate body Phillips saw the Confederates preparing to withdraw. At this point Phillips remounted his men, passed through the clearer land south of town, passed through town, and ended up to the left of Kelly to stop the anticipated rebel breakout.

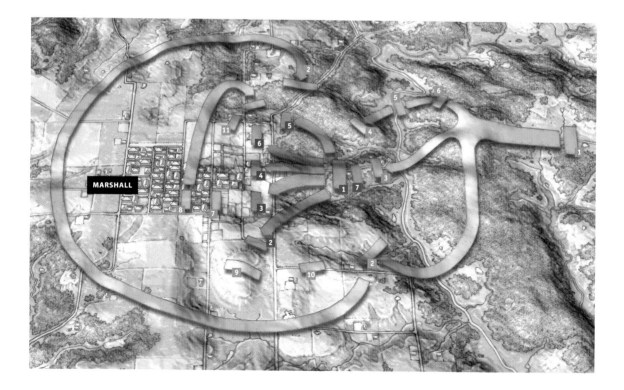

UNION FORCES 1 - 11

THE BATTLE OF MARSHALL

OCTOBER 13, 1863

BROWN'S FORCES

Total of 1,800 men and six pieces of artillery. Two six-pound guns under Capt Foster and four four-pound guns under Maj Houts.

1   BrigGen Egbert Brown

2   Col John F. Phillips: 800 men of the Seventh Missouri State Militia Cavalry

3   Maj T.W. Houts: 300 men and four pieces of artillery.

4   Capt Foster, followed by [**5**] Maj Suess and [**6**] Maj Foster and two pieces of artillery: 700 men

LAZEAR'S FORCES

1,020 men total. Two pieces of artillery.

7   LtCol B. F. Lazear and Maj A.W. Mullins: 300 men of the First Missouri State Militia Cavalry.

8   Maj G.W. Kelly: 200 men of the Fourth Missouri State Militia Cavalry

9   Maj J.H. McGhee: 200 men of the Second Battalion, First Missouri State Militia Cavalry

10 Capt W.D. Wear: 120 men of the Ninth Provisional Regiment Missouri State Militia Cavalry

11 Maj William Gentry: 200 men of the Fifth Provisional Regiment Missouri Enrolled Militia

STAGE TWO

Seeing he was outnumbered and flanked, Shanks made a fighting retreat towards the main rebel body with Houts harassing him the entire way. He never reached his commander, though, because Shelby mounted his force and prepared to break through the Union left and flee northwest. This maneuver took an hour because of the thick underbrush and many ravines and the need to build a bridge over one especially deep ravine so his wagons could cross. By the time he was ready to move out, Phillips had established his new position to the left of Kelly.

As Shelby moved out, Kelly remounted his men and charged, neatly cutting the rebel force in half. Shelby, Gordon, Coffee, and Elliot retreated to the northwest while Shanks, Hunter, and Hooper headed northeast. While Kelly's charge looks impressive on paper, in reality the two bodies of rebels had already been separated with only about twenty of Gordon's troops standing in Kelly's path. Kelly scattered them immediately and Phillips soon followed him into the gap. Shelby and his section of the rebel army were already headed northwest, and the rest of the rebels, under pressure from all sides, broke out in the other direction. Shelby had to pass through Gentry's militia, spread out to one man every six feet in order to cover both their section of the line and that formerly occupied by Kelly. Shelby's raiders scattered them easily, apparently with no loss on either side.

Phillips pursued Shelby's section for the rest of the day while Lazear moved his men west to intercept Shelby in case he turned south. Houts chased after the section of Shanks, Hunter, and Hooper. Both sections skirmished for the rest of the day with only light losses.

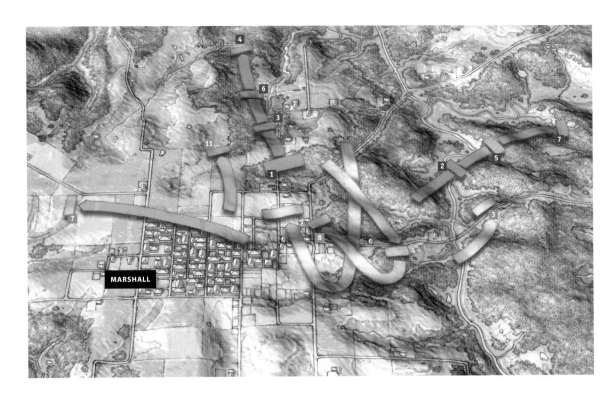

order to mount up, and for the rest of the night the raiders rode their jaded horses, passing through Waverly at three in the morning. There would be no homecoming for Shelby, however. He turned south without stopping, avoiding a concentration of troops 20 miles west at Lexington.

As the sun rose on October 14, Philips took up the trail once more. In minor local officers like Philips and Lazear, Shelby had met men of his own breed. They did not quit, nor did they satisfy themselves once Shelby had left their areas of control. Instead they led a dogged pursuit as exhausting as Shelby's retreat. Philips soon came upon the half-sunken wagons Shelby had

BrigGen John McNeil helped capture the State Guard at Camp Jackson and went on to become a successful guerrilla hunter. Missouri secessionists hated him for executing suspected spies and guerrillas, often on slim evidence. He successfully defended Cape Girardeau during Marmaduke's second raid, and chased Shelby during his Great Raid. He tangled with Shelby again during Price's raid in 1864. (LoC)

discarded the previous night. He knew that Shelby would be moving even faster than before and hurried his men on as one of his officers complained that it was "crazy work trying to catch a man who never stopped to eat or sleep."

On October 16 Shelby passed near Warrensburg, where Ewing had gathered 2,000 Union troops. Shelby stuck to the back paths and crept around the town, but was discovered just south of it near Johnstown. He fought Ewing off, losing one raider dead and several captured, and continued moving towards the Osage River, camping that night within 8 miles of it.

MajGen Schofield was determined to trap Shelby again. He ordered Brown to keep on Shelby's tail and skirmish with him. While Shelby was delayed with rearguard actions, McNeil would head north with 2,500 men and position himself along the Osage River to contest his crossing. He was to send scouts out along the 70 miles between Lebanon to Osceola to make sure the slippery raider didn't get by. Schofield wasn't about to underestimate Shelby, and if he did get by McNeil, Shelby would still have to deal with Ewing, who was ordered to move 1,000 men to Carthage, where he could strike out at any position in southwestern Missouri or northwestern Arkansas.

It was a good plan, but Shelby rode too hard for it to take effect. For the next two days he set a grinding pace – in one 18-hour period riding 108 miles – and made it to Carthage on the night of October 18 well before Ewing. Shelby's men rested here for part of the night before heading out again, but he gave Maj Pickler's men of Coffee's command permission to stay the entire night. Pickler's men were from Carthage and wanted to spend time with their families. Shelby always allowed this when he thought he could, because it was a boon to morale and the individuals so rewarded often received useful supplies.

This time it was a mistake. Pickler didn't post any pickets and got caught napping the next morning when Ewing's advance guard rode into town. After a brief fight, Pickler and 30 of his men were captured. Shelby heard the gunshots behind him and formed five companies into line to guard the retreat of the rest of his command. They put up a stubborn fight for an hour until Ewing unlimbered his artillery and forced them to withdraw. The chase continued.

Ewing sent a force around and ahead of Shelby to cut him off, but the raiders smacked into them and in a brief but fierce skirmish shoved them aside. Later that day Shelby came to the Wire Road leading from Springfield to Fayetteville and found a repair crew fixing the telegraph lines he'd cut on his way north. He captured the entire workforce and undid their repair job.

As Shelby and his men camped on the night of October 20, the scouts he had sent out ten days before joined up with him again. They'd been busy cutting telegraph wires, tearing up railroad tracks, and skirmishing with local Unionists. They brought in a good booty of 95 horses, five pack horses loaded with supplies, 73 Sharps rifles, 120 Colt Navy revolvers, and a dozen mules loaded with food.

Shelby and Hunter initially didn't realize they were camping only 5 miles apart, but their scouts soon found one another. Shelby was so happy to hear

**OCTOBER 15
1863**

Hunter fights at Cross Timbers

A brass 6-pdr smoothbore from the Chickamauga National Battlefield Park like the one Shelby brought on his raid. These were standard artillery pieces on both sides and this made them useful on raids since ammunition could be plundered from the enemy, although Shelby did not get the opportunity in this case. (Courtesy JackMelton.com)

Hunter had made it through that he mounted his weary horse and rode out to see him.

Horses and riders were now almost totally spent. Indeed they'd been leaving a trail of worn-out animals and men since Marshall. Shelby moved slowly from now on, choosing a zigzag path to elude his pursuers. For a time he avoided all opposition, but soon his scouts warned him that McNeil was chasing him with 1,000 men. Shelby was able to keep a lead on them until he reached the Boston Mountains on October 24, when the Federals finally caught up and Shelby was forced to fight a rearguard action all the way to Clarkesville on the Arkansas River on October 26. Crossing the river, he was almost home, but the region swarmed with alerted troops. Here was the last cordon of Union control before the no-man's land of central Arkansas and eventually rebel territory.

Luckily for him, the skies opened up with a terrible storm of freezing rain and snow. For six days his men struggled through it, looking over their shoulders for signs of Yankee pursuit. There was none; the Northerners had given up. On the sixth day Shelby and his men made it to his headquarters at Washington, Arkansas, and the raid was finished.

So were many of his men. During this entire chase, the Iron Brigade had been bleeding men. The Union pursuers were able to kill or capture a few at a time, but many more deserted or fell by the wayside, they and their mounts too exhausted to go on. It's impossible to say how many people Shelby lost at this stage as there is no precise record, and it's not known exactly how

The Charge of Shelby's Iron Brigade. (Andy Thomas, Artist. Carthage, Missouri www.andythomas.com)

many volunteers he picked up along the way. Edwards records 800, but that sounds like an estimate and a high one at that. The author of the Saline County history wrote that Confederate veterans told him Shelby had only 200 recruits at Marshall, half of whom were unarmed. It's doubtful that Shelby could have gathered many recruits after the battle, as he was in a race for his life. Recruits probably fell out more often than Iron Brigade veterans once they realized just what riding with J.O. Shelby entailed.

Edwards describes what it was like to go without sleep on one of these grueling rides:

> To those unacquainted with the effects produced by the loss of sleep, the sensations would be novel and almost incredible. About the third night an indescribable feeling settles down on the brain. Every sound is distinct and painfully acute. The air seems filled with exquisite music; cities and towns rise up on every hand, crowned with spires and radiant with ten thousand beacons. Long lines of armed men are on every side, while the sound of bugles and harsh words of command are incessantly repeated. Often, upon almost boundless prairies, destitute of tree or bush, the tormented dozer turns suddenly from some fancied oak, or mechanically lowers his head to avoid the sweeping and pendant branches. Beyond the third night stolid stupor generally prevails, and an almost total insensibility to pain. Soldiers in Shelby's division have been known to go incurably mad and not a few cases of hopeless idiocy have resulted from his terrible raids. On the march men have dropped from the saddle unawakened by the fall, while on more than a dozen occasions his rear guard has pricked the lagging sleepers with sabres until blood spouted, without changing a muscle on their blotched, bloated faces.

OCTOBER 20 1863

Shelby reunited with scouts and Hunter's column

This author himself can testify that for once in his life Edwards only exaggerated slightly. At about the same age as the youthful volunteers of the Iron Brigade, I spent three days and nights without sleep while crossing the desert between Pakistan and Iran. The first two nights were merely exhausting, not the least because of the constant watchfulness I had to keep on my poor choice of company. By the third night there was a general numbness, accompanied by tunnel vision. Strange, dark shapes flitted on the edge of my narrowed vision. For a man with such a hyperactive imagination and in such danger as Edwards, perhaps he really did see "cities and towns rise up on every hand."

These long marches actually ruined some people for life. Union captain George Grover recalled picking up stragglers from Shelby's retreat. "The rebels were in a pitiable plight, and many were demented, and in a dying condition, from hunger, exposure, loss of sleep, and terrific, long marching without rest." As Iron Brigade member Jake Stonestreet told a reporter long after the war, "No man could ride with Shelby for four years and be worth his salt at anything afterward. I did it and I know."

ANALYSIS

Shelby's raid, covering 1,500 miles in mostly enemy territory in 41 days, was one of the most remarkable actions of the war, yet it has never received the attention it warrants. The Civil War in the Trans-Mississippi theater has always been understudied by historians in favor of the bigger campaigns east of the Mississippi. Even the Union and Confederate high commands regarded the states west of the river as backwaters, only useful as a source of men and as a dumping ground for failed officers. What many observers then and now fail to notice is that the war west of the river was just as active and just as relevant as that in the more celebrated regions. A study of the Trans-Mississippi theater reveals some important aspects of military history, and students of the Civil War are now beginning to wake up to this fact. Several academic and popular presses are producing good studies of the campaigns and battles. Perhaps now J.O. Shelby and his Iron Brigade will receive the credit they are due.

"Rebel prisoners in dungeon of the state house at Jefferson City, Missouri." This engraving from *Harper's Weekly* shows the crowded conditions of Union prisons, but not the dirt and disease. Prisoners would be kept until they could be exchanged, but with the lull in regular operations in late 1863 through much of 1864, those rebels captured on Shelby's raid would have a long wait. Some fell ill and died before they got out. (LoC)

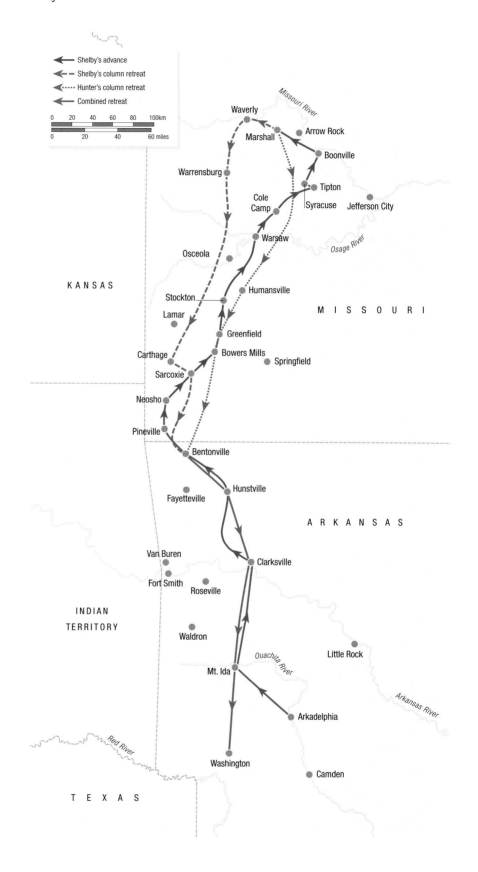

Shelby's raid of September
22 to October 26, 1863.

So how effective was the 1863 "Ride around Missouri," as veterans always called it? Like so many Confederate cavalry raids, it was well planned but proved to be only a moderate success. Shelby's main advantage was the disposition of the Union troops. The Federal, state, and local militia forces in Missouri were spread out to defend towns, bridges, and railroads from guerrillas. With no serious threat of invasion since early 1862, Missouri had been stripped of its most experienced units, leaving local militias to defend their home areas. The only real defense against a major invasion were Steele's forces along the Arkansas River valley. As we have seen, they were designed to block a slower moving army, not a quick raid. Even Price's ponderous 1864 "raid" of 12,000 men, dragging along a huge wagon train, had no trouble getting past this line.

While this disposition of troops made sense for an anti-guerrilla campaign, it had trouble dealing with a sizeable raiding force armed with cannon. Time and again Shelby snapped up small garrisons like a queen taking a row of pawns. In the grand scheme of things these little garrisons didn't mean much – most of their men fled or were paroled – but they provided the Confederates with much-needed supplies. Edwards reports they captured 40 stands of colors, 600 rifles of various types, 600 revolvers, 6,000 horses and mules, and a large quantity of uniforms. This is an impressive figure, even factoring in Edwards' usual hyperbole, although not on such a scale as to strengthen Confederate forces in Arkansas as a whole. Much of the booty, especially the worn-out horses, was probably left behind in the race for Arkansas. The official reports note that during their flight the raiders

Steamboats could deliver troops quickly and relatively safely. With the Union in control of the Mississippi and Missouri rivers, only fast raiding parties like Shelby's could hope to outmaneuver the Union army. (LoC)

OCTOBER 24 1863

Shelby fights rearguard action in Boston Mountains

A caricature of the "Southern Gentleman" on an illustrated Union envelope. Smoking a cheroot and drinking a mint julep, he seems hardly capable of raiding the pantry, let alone the North, yet many Southern gentlemen did just that, J.O. Shelby included. (LoC)

littered the road with plunder they'd picked up in Missouri. Capt Grover added that the rebels threw away "everything but guns."

The goal of disrupting Union operations in Missouri was spectacularly, if temporarily, achieved. Numerous blockhouses and bridges were burned, and the telegraph system stopped. The Union lost a fair amount of supplies as well, although these were quickly replaced. Edwards boasted that the damage cost the Union more than $2 million, but considering his overblown estimates of the cost of the Lamine railroad bridge this figure seems high. The Union casualties weren't great either – Edwards says 600, Federal sources are unclear but considerably lower – but inflicting casualties was not a goal of this or most raids.

Schofield, on the other hand, claimed that Shelby's retreat prompted many guerrillas to head south, "leaving behind a state of peace and security to which people have long been strangers." This may have been so, but as the leaves fell in the autumn and the underbrush provided less cover, guerrillas tended to go South for the winter anyway. Schofield may have been exaggerating this annual emigration to put his efforts in a better light.

Edwards says there were only 125 casualties among the raiders, but this figure seems low and may not count all the losses and desertions among the recruits. Union records cite numerous instances of Shelby's various pursuers picking up stragglers, although they don't say if these were veteran raiders or new recruits. In addition, Shelby had lost all his wagons and both his cannons.

Regarding another of Shelby's goals, that of recruiting men for the Southern cause, his raid was less successful. His column simply moved too quickly to mount a proper recruitment drive. Plus, by late 1863 most men who wanted to fight against the Union were already doing so, either in regular Confederate units or in one of the innumerable guerrilla bands. Edwards gives the number of recruits as 800, but it's unclear how many made it back to Arkansas. Some were killed or captured, and others dropped out from exhaustion or disillusionment along the way.

As far as lifting morale, Shelby succeeded brilliantly. Here, when all things looked dark, was a new hero to buoy the rebel spirit. Even though Missouri had been drained of most of its fighting men, the struggle continued there until the end of the war. It's also important not to underestimate the role of noncombatants. Older men, youths, and women supported rebel guerrillas and provided valuable intelligence to the Confederate army. They played a crucial role in supporting Price's invasion the following year. This renewal of popular support was in large part due to the charismatic leadership of J.O. Shelby. He may not have had the stature of a Forrest or a Morgan, but he was admired then and remembered today. As Price had promised, Shelby was promoted to brigadier-general in December 1863.

In his most important task, that of diverting forces from Rosecrans' Chattanooga campaign, Shelby also succeeded wonderfully. News came slow to the isolated rebel armies of the Trans-Mississippi theater, and Shelby didn't know that Rosecrans had been defeated at the battle of Chickamauga in Georgia two days before he set out on his raid. This grueling battle, the second bloodiest in the war after Gettysburg, sent Rosecrans' forces reeling back to Chattanooga, Tennessee, and into a siege. Confederate Gen Braxton Bragg's Army of Tennessee almost starved the defenders into submission before Grant came to the rescue. Rosecrans, his replacement George Thomas, and Grant himself were all in dire need of reinforcements to fight the tenacious Bragg, but while help came from all other quarters, virtually none came from Missouri. This was the direct result and intention of Shelby's raid.

Just the previous summer, Schofield had lent Grant 8,000 men to finish the siege of Vicksburg. Once the city fell these men returned to Missouri. When Schofield received a request for reinforcements on September 15, he refused to send a single man, citing his own need for reinforcements. When a second frantic request came on October 18, with Shelby riding free around the region, Schofield relented and sent one regiment and one battery of artillery.

In the end, Shelby's raid made no difference to the outcome of the war. While Bragg had the temporary advantage, his army had been bled dry at Chickamauga and in the ensuing weeks he was outfought, outmaneuvered, and outnumbered. Eventually he fled Tennessee altogether, leaving Georgia open for Sherman's "March to the Sea." Shelby could turn a flank or turn back steamboat traffic, but he could not turn the tide of history.

MajGen William Rosecrans was hailed as a military genius until his disastrous defeat at Chickamauga on September 19–20, 1863. Stopping reinforcements to Rosecrans was one of the main reasons for Shelby's raid. While Rosecrans was defeated prior to the raid, Shelby didn't know that until much later. With Rosecrans defeated and his army under siege in Chattanooga, reinforcements were needed more than ever. Like many other failed generals North and South, Rosecrans was transferred to the Trans-Mississippi theater, where he led the defense against Price's 1864 raid. (LoC)

AFTERMATH

OCTOBER 26 1863

Shelby crosses Arkansas River at Clarkesville

Shelby spent the winter of 1863/4 resting his men in Arkansas. There would be no more raids that season. The troops and horses were exhausted by their historic ride and had earned, and sorely needed, a long rest.

To the frustration of Confederate troops throughout the Trans-Mississippi, there were no offensive operations for much of 1864. MajGen Price, however, had come up with a grand scheme to retake Missouri. The November elections were fast approaching, and one of the sole remaining hopes for the beleaguered Confederacy was the candidacy of George McClellan. His Democratic Party was running on a peace ticket. McClellan himself had become a critic of the war and was gathering support among war-weary Northerners. While he said he wanted to continue the fight, his party's own opposition to it made him appear as a glimmer of hope to the South.

Kirby Smith and Sterling Price envisioned a bold plan. They reasoned that if Price made a strong thrust into Missouri and took the industrial and shipping center of St. Louis, it might tip the balance in favor of McClellan. A second objective was the state capital of Jefferson City. Missouri Confederate governor-in-exile Thomas Reynolds yearned to hold state elections in Missouri. Such a move, no matter how temporary, would give the Missouri Confederate government the legitimacy it craved and would prove embarrassing to Lincoln. They were encouraged by a line of Shelby's (really Edwards') report of the 1863 raid that said that the raiders had "found the people of Missouri as a mass, true to the South and her institutions, yet needing the strong presence of a Confederate army to make them volunteer."

Price gathered 9,000 men under himself and Generals Fagan and Marmaduke. Shelby and the Iron Brigade had already slipped across the Arkansas River and had spent the previous weeks scouring northern Arkansas, rounding up deserters and conscripting locals. This effort added 3,000 mostly unarmed men to Price's army, but they were of little value. Shelby reported he had "found the entire country overrun with able-bodied men; recruiting officers quarreling or sunk in total apathy; predatory bands of thieves roaming over the country at will, killing some, burning the feet of

NOVEMBER 3 1863

Shelby arrives back at his headquarters at Washington, Arkansas

others, and all hungering with the lust of robbery; one officer refusing to report to another, no organizations, no discipline, no arms, no leader, no desire to fight, no anything."

This description could have fitted many regions in the Trans-Mississippi. War weariness, lawlessness, and the near-collapse of the rural economy had left the land in chaos. Despite these ominous signs, Price rode on high hopes and entered Missouri on September 19. The rebels' first objective was the town of Pilot Knob, protected by Fort Davidson, in the lead-rich Arcadia valley in southern Missouri. Price hoped to capture the large supply of weapons and ammunition stored there. On September 27, waves of rebels advanced on the earthworks, only to get cut down by withering musket fire. The fort's many cannon cut bloody paths through the rebel ranks. But the Confederates pressed on, making it to the earthworks only to be fired upon at point-blank range. The defenders hurled crude grenades down on them, adding to the slaughter and forcing the rebels to retreat. They left more than a thousand of their comrades dead or dying in the fields around the fort.

That night the Union defenders managed to slip away and blow up the fort with powder triggered by a slow-burning fuze. Price had gained nothing. But he had lost something vital – time. The days spent besieging Fort Davidson and chasing the Union force, which eventually got away, allowed the North to reinforce St. Louis. Price decided he couldn't take it and headed for his secondary objective of Jefferson City. The ragtag rebel army marched

The Union defeat at the battle of Chickamauga, Tennessee, on September 19–20, 1863, ended MajGen Rosecrans' command of the Army of the Cumberland and nearly ended his career. After the defeat Union forces retreated into Chattanooga, where they were besieged by Gen Braxton Bragg. The siege was eventually broken by the arrival of Grant and a massive number of reinforcements. While Chickamauga was a Confederate victory, the rebel Army of Tennessee lost more than 18,000 men and never recovered. (LoC)

MajGen Sterling Price was beloved by his men but met with a string of defeats. Like Shelby, he never gave up hope of taking Missouri for the South. (LoC)

across Missouri, looting the countryside for food and other supplies. In mid October, Price reached Jefferson City only to find it protected by five forts. The rebels remembered their previous experience with fortified positions and didn't dare attack. While no one said the words, they began to realize they were no longer campaigning, but were in fact on the run.

They headed west along the Missouri River towards Kansas. Throughout this time, Shelby's men acted as vanguard or rearguard as the situation demanded, and sent out scouts to destroy infrastructure and determine enemy numbers. The rebels won several small battles and skirmishes in the central part of the state, but with their ranks swollen by refugees and untrained volunteers, their progress was slow and the Federals had time to organize. Coming up behind Price was a force of almost 14,000, while at the Kansas border there gathered an equally large army.

Price met the Kansans first, twice pushing them back, but the Kansans continued to fight a delaying action to let the army from St. Louis catch up. Price now faced the danger of being caught between two superior forces.

The three armies collided on October 23 at Westport, just southeast of Kansas City, in the largest battle west of the Mississippi. After a bloody fight, Price was able to get his men free of the noose, largely thanks to a bold charge by the Iron Brigade.

But Price's campaign had one more long, agonizing chapter before it could end. The Confederates entered Kansas pursued by Federal cavalry, who caught up with them at Mine Creek on October 25 and smashed through the Confederate lines, capturing 600 men and Gen Marmaduke. Only quick action by the Iron Brigade stopped the Union onslaught and saved the remainder of Price's army. The bulk of the rebels escaped in a disorderly and dispirited condition and without many of their supply wagons. Shelby fought another rearguard action near Newtonia on October 28, once again extricating Price's army intact. His men continued their weary way south as the weather worsened and added to their misery with rain, sleet, and snow. Many deserted.

The bedraggled army passed into the Indian Territory and the Northerners gave up the chase. But the nightmare wasn't over. The rebels had run out of food and resorted to eating horses and mules. Even generals had their horses stolen and put into the pot. Smallpox and other diseases ravaged the ranks. Some soldiers, having no blankets and only ragged clothing, simply froze to death. At this point, only the Iron Brigade remained a coherent unit. Shelby's strict but caring leadership and the men's own pride ensured that. In early December, Price made it back to Arkansas with only a few thousand men.

In retrospect, it seems doubtful Price could have taken St. Louis, but his invasion managed to divert 20,000 troops from the eastern campaigns, delaying Union advances in the East while causing a wave of fear among Northern sympathizers across the central states. The destruction of railways and supplies dealt a serious blow to the Union cause in Missouri, and Price's epic ride captured the imagination of the South. His army traveled 1,434 miles and fought 43 battles and skirmishes, making it one of the longest and hardest-fought campaigns in the Trans-Mississippi.

It was also the last gasp of the Confederacy west of the Mississippi. There would be no more offensives, and very little defensive action. Even the bushwhackers began to give up. Union countermeasures had improved, and more and more guerrillas fell victim to Federal bullets. Some rebels slipped back into the civilian population, or moved out West to start new lives. "Bloody Bill" Anderson had been shot while supporting Price's invasion. Quantrill was killed in the waning days of the war in Kentucky.

Kirby Smith saw the end had come and surrendered his men at Shreveport, Louisiana, on May 26, 1865. His was the last major Confederate army to surrender. Out in the Indian Territory, BrigGen Stand Watie, the only Native American general in the Confederacy, surrendered on June 23, becoming the last Confederate general to surrender.

But some did not give up. Romantics to the last, Shelby and his Iron Brigade, along with Governor Reynolds, Kirby Smith, Price, and other Confederate leaders of the Trans-Mississippi, rode south into Texas, headed for Mexico. They dreamed of carving out a new Confederacy from the chaos of the Mexican Civil War, or as the locals called it, The War of Reform. At the head of 600–1,000 hardcore veterans (the sources vary on the details, as in all episodes of his career) Shelby rode across Texas, quelling gangs of bandits and restoring law and order. At one point he retrieved a load of gold from a bank that had been robbed, killing all the robbers. Several local politicians and sheriffs tried to persuade the Iron Brigade to stay in their areas and protect them.

But the dream pulled them south. At the Rio Grande, Shelby sank his battle flag into the waters, along with the black plume that had become his trademark. At first the rebels considered joining the Juaristas, a peasant army fighting for land reform against the French puppet emperor Maximilian, who was defending traditional landed aristocracy and the interests of the Church. A run-in with a group of bandits allied with the Juaristas changed their minds, and the Iron Brigade sided with the emperor. Granted land, they formed the colony of Carlota near Vera Cruz. Maximilian proved to be another "Lost Cause," however, and was soon overthrown. The ex-Confederates held onto their land but the living proved harder than they expected. With the support of the government gone, the men longing for

Shelby and his men at Westport. The Iron Brigade was essential in Price's attempt to break out of the Union noose and escape back to Arkansas. (Andy Thomas, Artist. Carthage, Missouri www.andythomas.com)

home, and the realization that former rebels weren't being jailed or executed, members of the Iron Brigade began to drift back to the United States.

Shelby himself returned in 1867. He hadn't formally surrendered, and he never would. He once again took up farming and soon prospered, although he never reached the levels of wealth he had attained in the antebellum years. Like many other former Confederate leaders, he wisely avoided politics but loved Confederate reunions. Unlike his friend John Newman Edwards, however, his ardor for the "Lost Cause" slowly waned.

Near the end of Shelby's life, a Kansas historian asked him about his role in Bleeding Kansas, to which Shelby replied:

> I went there to kill Free State men. I did kill them. I am now ashamed of myself for having done so, but then times were different from what they are now, and that is what I went there for. We Missourians all went there for that purpose if it should be found necessary to carry out our designs. I had no business there. No Missourian had any business there with arms in his hands. The policy that sent us there was damnable and the trouble we started on the border bore fruit for ten years. I ought to have been shot there and John Brown was the only man who knew it and would have done it. I say John Brown was right. He did in his country what I would have done in mine in like circumstances. Those were the days when slavery was in the balance and the violence engendered made men irresponsible. I now see I was so myself.

In 1893 he was appointed US marshal for Missouri's Western District, where the following year he quelled a Pullman strike that had blocked the railroad.

St. Louis was not only an important industrial and shipping center, but also a shipyard for building gunboats. This 1861 engraving shows the gunboat *New Era* under construction. Taking St. Louis was a central Confederate goal for many officers in the Trans-Mississippi, but they never got enough support from Richmond to make a serious attempt on the city. (LoC)

"Poor deluded Miss-Souri takes a Secession bath, and finds it much hotter than she expected!" The Civil War in Missouri was hot for both sides. Tens of thousands of civilians were displaced, hundreds or perhaps thousands killed by violence or exposure, and much of the countryside was laid waste. (LoC)

Poor deluded Miss-Souri takes a Secession bath, and finds it much hotter than she expected!

Shelby used a force made up of equal numbers Iron Brigade and Union veterans. When Missouri governor William Stone criticized him for bringing Federal influence to bear on state politics, Shelby replied that the issue had been settled at Appomattox. The Confederate had become an American, and remained one until his death in 1897.

CONCLUSION

Daniel O'Flaherty, the only historian to write a full-length biography of Shelby, wrote: "It was Shelby's fate that his cavalry genius was used over and over again merely to save Confederate armies from the destruction invited by the military incompetence of his superiors." This is certainly a correct assessment. It could also be said that Shelby was a victim of geography. If he had stayed in Kentucky like his friend John Hunt Morgan, he would have fought in the more famous theaters of the Civil War east of the Mississippi. His abilities would probably have been recognized earlier and he would have been given a greater opportunity to help the Confederate war effort.

Shelby performed an invaluable service to the Trans-Mississippi cavalry. Union major-general Alfred Pleasonton said Shelby was the greatest Confederate cavalry officer of them all, and this from a man who had faced J.E.B. Stuart. Pleasonton wasn't the only Union veteran to praise Shelby. Capt George Grover, in a speech about the raid to his old army friends, stated bluntly that "If it had been in Virginia or Tennessee it would have been called one of the great campaigns of the Civil War."

The gray-haired Confederate veterans of the war west of the Mississippi would certainly have agreed. They used to boast, "You've heard of Jeb Stuart's ride around McClellan? Hell, brother, Shelby rode around MISSOURI!"

Despite what the epitaph says, the long-lived Pvt John Thomas Graves was actually the second-to-last of Shelby's men; he was actually the last resident at the Confederate Soldiers Home at Higginsville, MO. The last living man to have served with Shelby was Joseph Hayden Whitsett, who died in 1951. For the generation who knew these aged veterans, the American Civil War is still within living memory. (Sean McLachlan)

BIBLIOGRAPHY

Bird, Roy, "JO Shelby and his Shadow" in *America's Civil War*, Vol. 8, No. 1 (March 1995) pp.26–32

Britton, Wiley, *The Civil War on the Border*, Vols I & II, G.P. Putnam's Sons, New York (1899), reprinted by Kansas Heritage Press, Ottawa (1994)

Castel, Albert, *General Sterling Price and the Civil War in the West*, Louisiana State University Press, Baton Rouge (1996)

Christensen, Lawrence O., William E. Foley, Gary R. Kremer, and Kenneth H. Winn (eds), *Dictionary of Missouri Biography*, University of Missouri Press, Columbia (1999)

DeBlack, Thomas A., *With Fire and Sword: Arkansas, 1861–1874*, University of Arkansas Press, Fayetteville (2003)

Denny, James M., "Civil War Entrenchment at the Lamine River Railroad Bridge near Otterville" in the *Mid-Missouri Civil War Roundtable Newsletter*, http://mmcwrt.missouri.org/2000/default0008.htm (accessed Jan 25, 2011)

Denny, James M., "The Battle of Marshall: The Greatest Little Battle that Was Never Fought" in the *Mid-Missouri Civil War Roundtable Newsletter*, http://mmcwrt.missouri.org/2001/default0112.htm (accessed Nov 9, 2010)

Edwards, John Newman, *Shelby and His Men* (1867), reprinted 1993 General Joseph Shelby Memorial Fund, Waverly, Missouri

Goman, Frederick W., *Up From Arkansas: Marmaduke's First Missouri Raid including the Battles of Springfield and Hartville*, Wilson's Creek National Battlefield Foundation, Springfield, Missouri (1999)

Grover, George S., "The Shelby Raid, 1863" in *Missouri Historical Review*, Vol. 6, No. 3 (April 1912) pp.107–126

Hosier, Scott, "'JO' Shelby goes home to Missouri" in *America's Civil War*, Vol. 15, No. 6 (January 2003) pp.34–42

Johnson, William F., *History of Cooper County, Missouri*, Historical Publishing Company, Topeka, Kansas (1919)

Kerby, Robert L., *Kirby Smith's Confederacy: The Trans-Mississippi South, 1863–1865*, University of Alabama Press, London (1972)

Leslie, Edward E., *The Devil Knows How to Ride: The True Story of William Clarke Quantrill and his Confederate Raiders*, Da Capo Press, New York (1996)

McLachlan, Sean, *American Civil War Guerrilla Tactics*, Osprey Publishing, Oxford (2009)

McLachlan, Sean, *Missouri: An Illustrated History*, Hippocrene Books, New York (2008)

Missouri Historical Company, *History of Saline County*, St. Louis, Missouri (1881)

Oates, Stephen B., *Confederate Cavalry West of the River*, University of Texas Press, Austin (1961)

O'Flaherty, Daniel, *General JO Shelby: Undefeated Rebel*, University of North Carolina Press, Chapel Hill & London (2000)

Scott, Mark E., *The Fifth Season: General "JO" Shelby's Great Raid of 1863*, Two Trails Publishing, Independence, Missouri (n.d.)

Sellmeyer, Deryl P., *JO Shelby's Iron Brigade*, Pelican Publishing Company, Gretna, Louisiana (2007)

US War Department, *The War of the Rebellion: A Compilation of the Official Records of the Union and Confederate Armies*, Government Printing Office, Washington, DC (1888)

Overgrown boys having fun? Well, yes, but Shelby's 5th Missouri Cavalry is actually reenacting a common practice of 19th-century America. Riding into a shop or a saloon was a young man's way of showing off, and with a good supply of weaponry he was sure to get a drink. (From the collection of Scott Hughes)

INDEX

Figures in **bold** refer to illustrations